Living with Extreme

In *Living with Extreme Intelligence: Developing Essential Communication Skills*, Dr Sonja Falck provides a unique and practical manual of how to improve interactions that involve adults who stand out from the neurotypical majority by having top 2% IQ. Her main message is that understanding the individual differences involved in extreme intelligence and mastering relevant communication skills can break through barriers of frustration, underachievement, and loneliness, to bring about brain-changingly positive conversations and interpersonal effectiveness, connection, and joy.

Dr Falck begins by explaining the neurophysiological and social foundations of why we communicate the way we do and then explains in detail seven essential communication skills. Following this, she shows how to put these skills into practice, applying insights from depth psychology and demonstrating how to have better conversations in a variety of contexts from general social gatherings to the workplace and intimate relationships.

Particular attention is paid to areas that Dr Falck's research and professional practice have repeatedly shown her are challenging for adults with extreme intelligence, such as small talk, office politics, dating, and handling conflict. She draws on case examples from her consulting work (psychotherapy and coaching) with clients who have extreme intelligence, and examples from novels, cinema, the media, the literature on giftedness, and biographical material on high-profile high-IQ figures like Steve Jobs, Elon Musk, and Lady Gaga. Throughout she emphasises the theme from her original model of interpersonal relating, which is that experiencing freedom of self-expression with others who offer you a high level of acceptance is what puts you in a state of thriving.

The book provides step-by-step guidance for engaging in numerous interpersonal situations, such as how to handle difficult conversations, how to write effective emails, how to breathe, listen, play, take a risk, bond, repair a broken connection, and keep yourself well through changes like failure, success, and falling in love. It is essential reading for anyone affected by, or interested in, issues associated with extremely high intelligence.

Sonja Falck is a Senior Lecturer at the University of East London. She is author of *Extreme Intelligence* and *The Psychology of Intelligence*. She is a psychotherapist and supervisor accredited with the UKCP and BACP, specialising in improving personal and professional relationships. She has presented her work in Britain, the USA, and Holland.

Living with Extreme Intelligence

Developing Essential Communication Skills

Sonja Falck

Routledge
Taylor & Francis Group

LONDON AND NEW YORK

Designed cover image: Zea Eagle

First published 2023
by Routledge
4 Park Square, Milton Park, Abingdon, Oxon OX14 4RN

and by Routledge
605 Third Avenue, New York, NY 10158

Routledge is an imprint of the Taylor & Francis Group, an informa business

© 2023 Sonja Falck

British Library Cataloguing-in-Publication Data
A catalogue record for this book is available from the British Library

ISBN: 9780367464998 (hbk)
ISBN: 9780367464974 (pbk)
ISBN: 9781003029106 (ebk)

DOI: 10.4324/9781003029106

Typeset in Bembo
by Apex CoVantage, LLC

This book is dedicated to:

My sons, Damon and Lawrence – both of you are already wonderful communicators, and it is my greatest pleasure to watch you thriving.

and

My sisters, Zea and Esther – over the years we have had such great times together and fought so hard with each other that this helped me work out how better to increase the great times and avoid the fights.

Contents

'Do try this at home' – list of end-of-chapter boxouts

Illustrations

Table

Figures

Preface

The first time I started thinking very deliberately about the importance of effective communication was when – as a brave, or foolish, young South African graduate – I did a lot of hitchhiking around the world. It seemed to me that the reason most people would give me a ride was because they wanted to *talk* and that communicating carefully and effectively during such a high-risk method of travel is what earned me my transportation as well as my safety.

During my travels, I kept noticing the power and pleasure of talking that transcends the variants of country and culture. Sitting chatting with fellow travellers in Mexico on a beach in the small hours one morning, giant cacti silhouetted against the bright low moon, I asked a Swede to let me hear him speak his mother tongue (I didn't understand Swedish).

He started talking, hesitantly at first, then relaxed into it. Soon he asked in English, 'Are you sure you can't understand my words?'

I replied, 'No – why?'

He said, 'Because you're listening so intently, like you're very absorbed in what I'm saying'. He continued in Swedish.

A bit later he switched back to English and said, 'I've never talked so freely to anyone before, never expressed myself so intensely. I'm only talking about how beautiful I find the changing seasons, but I'm saying it very emotionally, in a way I would otherwise find embarrassing, how much I *love* the autumn leaves'.

This is how I began to understand that the experience and effects of conversation also transcend the meanings of words – there is something important about the process of conversation that is distinct from the content of what is said.

I no longer hitchhike, relying on effective communication to earn me a method of transport. Instead, for all the many years since those original travels of mine, I have relied on effective communication to earn me my entire living. In my profession as a psychotherapist – and in my work as an executive coach and my academic post as a lecturer – talking is what earns me my income.

What still fascinates me is these two main principles: how listening in the right way can unlock unexpected adventures in interpersonal experience, and how talking freely in the presence of an absorbed and accepting listener – expressing the full intensity of what you feel and how you see the world, without embarrassment – promotes joy, healing, growth, and better relation-ships. How good conversation positively changes our brains, with long-lasting effects, has been demonstrated with research published in places like the Harvard Business Review.[1]

And yet, I came to discover that conversation could unfortunately become something more problematic than pleasurable when an individual difference was involved that I have called extreme intelligence. This was a prominent theme I encountered in my doctoral research. I presented this in my first book, *Extreme Intelligence – Development, Predicaments, Implications*, but found I had much more material about this than could fit into one book.

Also, in my professional practice I was experiencing day to day that a regular topic of focus in sessions with very high-IQ clients was their difficulties with interpersonal communication. Through all of this I started developing ideas about how to conceptualise what was difficult and how to address it to help make it better.

I realised there was a demand for information like this. British Mensa advertised to its members a talk by me titled 'The Three Vital Communication Skills for High-IQ Individuals', and all the 120 available tickets sold out within an hour of it being advertised. At that talk, in the lift afterwards, one of the attendees said to me: 'But we need more examples of how to actually do this'. Following that I received emails from Mensa members in other countries who had heard about my talk asking whether I could point them to any publications of the talk's content.

The current book is that publication, incorporating and elaborating on the content from that successful Mensa presentation. (What in that talk I called the 'three vital' skills are in this book called the 'top three' skills out of a total of seven skills that I present – see Chapters 4 and 5.) My first book explained the nature of, and reason there might be, interpersonal difficulty where extreme intelligence is involved, and the current book focuses on what you can do about it, with lots of examples. My wish for you is that reading this book will bring better conversations into your life and help you thrive.

Reference

Glaser, J.E. and Glaser, R.D. (2014). The Neurochemistry of Positive Conversations. [online] *Harvard Business Review*. Available at: https://hbr.org/2014/06/the-neurochemistry-of-positive-conversations [Accessed 16 July 2022].

Acknowledgements

This book draws on innumerable valuable conversations I have had the benefit of participating in with my family, friends, colleagues, clients, and students. There are far too many individuals to mention, and many who I gave the option of being mentioned have expressed their preference for anonymity. I thank you all.

I am grateful to my colleagues at the University of East London for many different ways in which they supported my writing, including Dr Fenia Christodoulidi, Dr Lucia Berdondini, Dr Paul Galbally, and Dr Max Eames. I thank my international colleagues, including Dr Jerald Grobman, and Rianne van de Ven. A special mention to my friends Dr Laine Jaderberg, Cathy Bawlf, and Tony Noguera.

Thank you to Tomasz Namielski, who took the picture I had hand-drawn for my students and wonderfully converted it to a much more professional-looking version (see Chapter 8, Figure 8.1).

My special gratitude goes to Zea Eagle and Judith Balcazar for reading my draft manuscript and providing valuable critique and associated stimulating conversations. I further thank Zea Eagle for collaborating with me to create another beautiful original artwork for the book's cover and for her unfailing interest, involvement, research assistance, and wise insights that have richly supported my learning and writing.

Thank you to my editors at Routledge, Emilie Coin and Khyati Sanger, for all the usual work your roles involve plus a lot of extra kindness and flexibility, which has been a great help to me and much appreciated.

Thank you to Michael Owen, who has made me fall in love all over again with the profound work of being a psychotherapist.

Thank you to Damon Falck for suggesting a writing retreat for me in Oxford and all your personalised recommendations for daily libraries and coffee shops to try – this gave me an unforgettable week of full-time writing in one of the world's most iconic cities devoted to thinking and learning and writing. Thank you to my husband Richard Harding for holding the fort at home to allow me the week in Oxford and for all round being my muse, companion, playmate, and collaborator. Thank you to Lawrence Falck for your usual forbearance while I write – you endured far too many takeaways (though it's funny how happy you always seemed about that!).

Introduction

On the cover of this book a cheetah runs through flames and shatters glass. It is an original artwork by Zea Eagle entitled *Breaking Barriers*, specially created for the book. The cheetah represents people who have extreme intelligence, referencing an article well known in the world of giftedness that likened being gifted to being a cheetah.[2] And the main message of this book is that good communication can help you break through barriers.

Defining extreme intelligence

My definition of extreme intelligence is general cognitive ability in humans that is higher than that of at least 98% of the general population. The traditional method of measuring this is with IQ tests, and on most standardised IQ tests this would translate into a score of 130 or higher. This is also the range that the term 'giftedness' refers to in the academic and research literature and which often forms the threshold for gaining entrance to specialised gifted educational programmes.

Because of the overlaps in meaning between the terms 'extreme intelligence', 'gifted', 'very high IQ', and 'high ability', in my writing I use all these terms for the phenomenon I am dealing with. The phenomenon is essentially brain structure and function that is different from that of the majority of the general population (therefore it can correctly be called a neurodivergence or neuroatypicality) in a way that gives rise to high ability and heightened intensity of experience which stand out as different from the majority. I say more about this in Chapter 1, and indeed the whole book discusses and elaborates on this in various ways throughout. But if you would like to read more background and explanation of this, together with an in-depth presentation of the many issues and debates surrounding this phenomenon, please see my book *Extreme Intelligence*.[3] There I also discuss how the terms 'intelligence', 'giftedness', 'expertise', and 'genius', and their respective fields of research, relate to each other.[4] If you would like a historical contextualisation of how Western society conceptualises human intelligence and the psychology underlying the way we respond to human intelligence, please see my book *The Psychology of Intelligence*.[5]

DOI: 10.4324/9781003029106-1

The current book's title – *Living with Extreme Intelligence* – intentionally evokes three possible interpretations, showing that it is about:

1   Living with your own extreme intelligence.
2   Living with others who have extreme intelligence.
3   Living in a way that is extremely intelligent.

The first two interpretations recognise that biopsychosocial individual differences exist between persons who have very high IQ and those who do not, and that all concerned can benefit from learning about these differences and implementing relevant skills to make communication and collaboration with each other more effective. The third interpretation of the title suggests that applying the book's ideas and guidelines will promote a way of living that is extremely intelligent.

Difficulties in communication

A factor that can make communicating with someone else a struggle is when there are large differences between you in your respective ways of functioning, particularly when you are unaware this is the case and don't know what's involved or what to do about it. Although any two people can have trouble communicating with each other at any point, and therefore the principles I present in this book are relevant to anyone, I am also specifically addressing the kinds of interpersonal difficulty that commonly arise when the neurodivergence of extreme intelligence is involved.

The term 'neurodivergent' or 'neuroatypical' is often associated with autism. Autism spectrum disorder (ASD)[6] is classed as a developmental disability, and the hallmark feature of ASD is difficulty with interpersonal communication. There has been research that suggests there are higher rates of ASD in very high-IQ populations.[7] When someone with ASD also has high IQ, this is sometimes referred to as 'high-functioning autism', which used to be called Asperger's Syndrome. It is also termed twice exceptionality, or 2e, when a person has two or more kinds of atypical individual differences present simultaneously.

I have found in my research, in the literature, and in my consulting work, that the interpersonal problems individuals with extreme intelligence experience can be similar to ASD experiences, such as not having the same stamina for and interest in social communication that neurotypical individuals ordinarily have, nor the same capacity for accurately interpreting its various nuances and intuiting how to respond appropriately. Sometimes this is because a genuine developmental disability is present, but sometimes it is simply because the person has not been exposed to the kind of guidance that would facilitate learning these skills. Also, individuals with extreme intelligence might only experience these difficulties when communicating with neurotypical others, finding that interpersonal interaction becomes exponentially easier when they are with similar others who also have very high IQ like themselves.

I have worked with some extremely intelligent clients who decided to seek an assessment for ASD, and who received a positive diagnosis. They had many different thoughts and feelings associated with this which they discussed with me at length. Those who did this have ultimately found the diagnosis helpful and even a relief as it made sense for them of a lot of their experience and helped them find a better way of living with that individual difference.

This does not mean that every extremely intelligent person would, if assessed, receive a positive diagnosis of ASD. It also does not mean that whenever a diagnosis of ASD is given, it is correct. Much has been written about misdiagnosis, and also about missed diagnosis.[8]

Many of my clients never mention ASD to me, or mention it but have never sought an assessment, or have discussed with me that they would not want an assessment. I see any prospect of assessment for an adult as being a personal choice for the individual concerned. In my practice I do not myself administer tests for IQ or ASD, and I never require clients to undertake any such tests. If they decide they want such a test I can signpost them to where to get one.

I have found that even when an adult with extreme intelligence gains a diagnosis of ASD, they do not find it easy to find resources that would be helpful for them. Many ASD resources are not differentiated to be suitable for those with extreme intelligence and are much too simplistic. The current book focuses on communication skills specifically relevant for extremely intelligent individuals – whether or not they have any other additional individual difference simultaneously present – and those around them who might find this helpful.

The clients I work with

Within my professional practice I work with many clients whose personal experience resonates with issues related to extreme intelligence, in themselves and/or in a loved one or in someone they work with, regardless of whether any tests have been taken or their outcome. I have found that there are typical themes in the experiences and difficulties that adults with extreme intelligence encounter and which they describe to me.

But beyond these similar themes, such individuals are as different from each other as any human beings can be from each other. They come to me at various ages and stages of life and from many different walks of life, from diverse backgrounds, nationalities, and ethnicities, and they bring me challenges in living that range from the highly personal (from how to find a partner and begin their first sexual relationship – sometimes at ages well beyond what is developmentally typical – to going through crises in marriage or parenthood, or undergoing fertility treatment to become a lone parent) to the professional (from university students dealing with high pressure and career choices, to more mature adults addressing difficulties at work or seeking development within their career or grappling with a change in or end of career).

Whoever my clients are and whatever they bring to me, I think there are three main dimensions involved:

1   *Basic humanity* – the commonalities among us as fellow members of the human species (such as that we are genetically designed to seek safety and belonging).
2   *Extreme intelligence* – a biopsychosocial individual difference that affects a minority of humans.
3   *Communication* – the way we interact with each other, which is the basis of every personal and professional relationship within human existence.

Working with my clients to better understand each of these three dimensions and how they manifest for them individually will also help them with whatever issue they are facing.

Originality of this book

A key finding in my research and professional consulting work to date is that a significant proportion of extremely intelligent/very high IQ/gifted individuals find interpersonal communication problematic. And yet, I have not found a book that is fully dedicated to addressing this issue in adults.

There are books on (neurotypical) communication in general, and books on communication related to gifted children and teens, and books on communication for those on the autistic spectrum. None of these resources specifically target, nor are therefore specifically suitable for, adults who have extreme intelligence.

Also, although there are overlaps in content, none of these books has conceptualised the difficulty in communication or how it can be tackled in quite the same way I have found myself doing through my psychotherapy and coaching work. In week-by-week sessions many very high-IQ adults explain to me the problems they experience and ask for my help with what to do about them. I have wanted to try to put down in a book some of the main ideas I've developed and the knowledge I draw on when working with them, and some stories about how this has helped, so that more people can have access to this than the number I am able to personally work with one hour at a time in consulting sessions.

Feedback from international peer reviews of my work has highlighted that the originality and value of my work lie in its focus on the psychosocial implications associated with giftedness/high IQ/extreme intelligence and the fact I am a practitioner consulting within this growing field.

Who is this book for?

The main point of this book is to explicate the foundations, skills, and practice of effective communication specifically where extreme intelligence is involved.

It is designed to assist anyone interested in or affected by extreme intelligence to improve interpersonal communication in their daily personal and professional lives.

In writing the book, I have set myself the challenge of trying to make it readable to any interested adult, but also complex enough to be relevant and stimulating to more specialised readers who have a greater level of existing knowledge and experience in related fields. I have therefore also broached some more sophisticated topics but in easy-to-access language. Areas of knowledge I draw on in my writing include Relational Psychoanalysis, Attachment Theory, Polyvagal Theory, Transactional Analysis, Systemic thinking, and Dialectical Behaviour Therapy.

I therefore see this book as being relevant to the following kinds of readers:

- General interested readers.
- Members of organisations and businesses that employ individuals with high ability.
- Individuals affected by high IQ, such as members of high-IQ societies, and parents of and others involved with children identified as gifted.
- Students of psychology, counselling, and psychotherapy, and other related social sciences.
- Practitioners and tutors within these disciplines.
- People studying intelligence and individual differences in Further or Higher Education.
- Trainees and practitioners in general education and in gifted education.
- Continuing Professional Development attendees in psychiatry, psychology, psychotherapy, social work, and education.
- Readers interested in or professionally involved in the subject of interpersonal communication.
- Those affected by or working with ASD.

My writing comes from a perspective influenced by the country and era within which I live and work, but the book's subject is relevant to all human beings and should remain so into the long-distant future, because communicating with others is a universal and perennial need and developing skills for becoming more effective at getting along with others will always be helpful.

Structure of the book

The book is divided into three parts, related respectively to introducing the foundations of communication (three chapters), then explaining the specific skills I am presenting (two chapters), and then showing how the skills can be put into practice in various contexts (five chapters).

Part I – Foundations – introduces the fundamentals involved in basic and more advanced communication, with an emphasis on aspects salient to those with very high IQ. Part I thereby also lays the foundations for the book as these fundamentals will be referred back to throughout the rest of the book. Chapter 1 begins by explaining the neurophysiological basis of communication, how communication is of central importance in the life of the human mammal, and how we are born with a strong drive to seek safety and connection with others that continues to affect us throughout our lives. Chapter 2 demonstrates how some of these principles manifest when two people interact, by presenting and analysing a conversation I had with a Mensa member who is a barrister. This introduces some of the complications that can trip up the interpersonal communication of a person who has extreme intelligence. Chapter 3 explains how some of these interpersonal conundrums can be formulated as 'games' people play. It discusses how the alienating effects of such games can lead to social avoidance and explains authentic relating as the antidote to this. Different ways of playing are discussed, arguing for the usefulness at times of 'playing along' and the value of recovering/cultivating 'the art of play' in adulthood.

Moving from the general to the specific, Part I's foundations of underlying principles make way for a focus on the step-by-step details of the phases and skills involved in cycles of communication. Part II – Skills – explains seven essential communication skills (Chapter 4), together with an acronym for remembering these, and then goes deeper by elaborating the top three of the seven skills (Chapter 5).

Part III – Practice – addresses the question of how to have better conversations. It takes the overall foundational concepts and communication skills presented in the first two parts of the book and demonstrates how these can be implemented in various contexts of interpersonal interaction from the personal to the professional. It covers areas that my research and consulting work have repeatedly shown me are tricky for individuals with very high IQ, such as small talk (addressed in Chapter 6 as part of an overview of general conversation), dating and romance (addressed as part of intimate conversations discussed in Chapter 8), and office politics (included within Chapter 9's focus on occupational conversation). Chapter 7 engages with the subject of difficult conversations in different contexts and the principles of conflict resolution. Chapter 10 looks at change, especially concerning the gaining of success.

Finally, a concluding chapter provides comments that consolidate the main message of the book, which is that understanding the individual differences involved in extreme intelligence and mastering related effective communication skills can break through barriers of frustration, underachievement, and loneliness, to bring about connection, joy, and fulfilment.

Do try this at home

At the end of every chapter there is a boxout titled 'Do try this at home'. Each one relates to that chapter's content, and offers material such as skills, tips, questions for reflection, and instructions that are designed to aid readers to apply something in their own lives that is relevant to the chapter's learning.

Each chapter also includes a full reference list of any published sources referred to in the chapter.

Notes

1 Glaser and Glaser (2014).
2 Tolan (1996).
3 Falck (2020).
4 Falck (2020) – see the Introduction. This explains the Bell Curve of human intelligence, includes a section on 'The language of intelligence and related concepts' (pp. 3–5), and provides a diagram that shows how the different concepts relate to each other (p. 4, 'Figure 0.2 – Potential and performance').
5 Falck (2021).
6 See American Psychiatric Association (2013).
7 See Crespi (2016).
8 For example, see Webb et al. (2016).

References

American Psychiatric Association. (2013). *Diagnostic and Statistical Manual of Mental Disorders: DSM-5* (5th ed.). Washington, DC: American Psychiatric Publishing.

Crespi, B.J. (2016). Autism as a Disorder of High Intelligence. *Frontiers in Neuroscience*, [online] 10(300). doi:10.3389/fnins.2016.00300.

Falck, S. (2020). *Extreme Intelligence – Development, Predicaments, Implications*. London: Routledge.

Falck, S. (2021). *The Psychology of Intelligence*. London: Routledge.

Tolan, S.S. (1996). *Is It a Cheetah?* [online]. Available at: www.stephanietolan.com/is_it_a_cheetah.htm [Accessed 14 August 2022].

Webb, J.T., Amend, E.R., Beljan, P., Webb, N.E., Kuzujanakis, M., Olenchak, F.R. and Goerss, J. (2016). *Misdiagnosis and Dual Diagnoses of Gifted Children and Adults* (2nd ed.). Tucson, AZ: Great Potential Press.

Part I

Foundations

The fundamentals involved in basic
and more advanced communication

1 All people seek safety and connection (why we communicate the way we do)

Imagine you're talking to someone, and they stick their fingers in their ears. How would you feel? What would you think?

Chances are you'd feel surprised. And perhaps hurt, or offended. You're likely to experience it as that person wanting to block you out.

You might think the person is inappropriate and rude (this would be called an other-attribution). Or maybe you'd think you must have been talking rubbish (a self-attribution) and so they were right to realise this and shut you out.

In this situation, what would you do? Would you say something combative? Walk away? Might you go silent and physically still, your mind blank, or start thinking of something else as though you're not even there anymore?

What you would do depends on many things, such as how you interpreted the person's actions, your personality, the social status of that person compared with your own, what the relationship is between you, the context within which the conversation is taking place, and what the environment around you is like. If you are two good friends joking together at a party then you might find them sticking their fingers in their ears funny and start laughing.

All the reactions I've mentioned are based on assumptions that are typical in Western societies. One of these assumptions is that the person who sticks their fingers in their ears has voluntarily chosen to do that. Another assumption is that they had a psychological motivation for behaving that way. This could be – if looking at the specifics of the situation – that they are rejecting what you're saying, or – if generalising to a universal judgement – that they're rejecting you as a whole person.

These assumptions rest on a further assumption, which is that if someone behaves this way while in conversation with you, it has something to do with you. Whether you make an other-attribution or self-attribution, and whether you stay with the specifics of the situation or jump to a generalisation, you're thinking they stuck their fingers in their ears because of their conversation with you. In other words, you're responding self-referentially, taking it personally.

Now, if I told you this incident did happen, and it was a parent talking and a child sticking their fingers in their ears, how would you react? Your reaction would have a lot to do with your culture and the kind of family you grew up

DOI: 10.4324/9781003029106-3

in. All cultures have strong ideas about how parents and children should behave with each other.

What if I told you this incident happened not just once with this person, this child, but repeatedly? Then how would you view it?

In everything I've covered so far, maybe you've spotted something crucial that hasn't been considered. What's been left out is the central role played in all interpersonal communication by the physiology of our bodies, via the autonomic nervous system.

The central impact of your autonomic nervous system[1] on all your communication

'Autonomic' means involuntary. Each of us has a complex network of nerve cells and fibres which transmits nerve impulses between parts of our bodies. Right from the start of life, our primary need is to survive, and therefore a primary function of our nervous systems is to detect potential danger and act to restore safety. This is an involuntary process: we are genetically programmed to seek safety because our survival depends on being safe.

To have a conversation with someone requires the smooth operation of what has been termed our 'Social Engagement System'.[2] This is a group of neural pathways that connects the face with the heart, coordinating the heart with the muscles of the face and head. It coordinates facial expressions, like smiling, and vocalisations, like talking and singing. It also coordinates breathing and sucking and swallowing. Atypical coordination of this system early in life predicts later difficulties in social behaviour.[3]

Movement in the upper facial muscles and a voice that expressively goes up and down in pitch – termed 'prosody' – are associated with being socially connected and relaxed. Low movement in these facial muscles and a monotone voice that lacks prosody indicate a depressed Social Engagement System, meaning that the person is not feeling safe. Lack of upper-face movement is the typical facial presentation of someone who is suffering from trauma. It is also the facial presentation of someone who has had Botox.

Animated facial expressions and a prosodic voice are not only how we behave when we feel safe but also what we react to in others as cues that they are safe to be with. A mother typically speaks reassuringly to her baby with exaggerated facial expressions and prosody – a liltingly sing-song voice. The sci-fi television series Star Trek brilliantly created the exact opposite of this in how they designed a futuristic enemy most ultimately terrifying to humanity, called the Borg. Members of the Borg have frozen faces devoid of natural expressive movement, and they speak in a low-frequency monotonous voice with no prosody, sounding robotic. All of these are primitively visceral danger cues. (We are hard-wired to associate low-frequency sounds with danger because the rustle through undergrowth and growl of a stalking predator are low-frequency sounds.[4])

We detect safety versus danger through our senses, such as in the visual and auditory ways already described. But our nervous systems also detect such cues at an automatic and unconscious level, termed 'neuroception'.[5] This occurs at the level of reflex, an involuntary reaction outside of our conscious control. If we touch a hot stove, we have the instant reflex of pulling our hand away from the source of heat, to avoid being burnt. If we eat something that makes us feel ill, we develop an instant taste aversion to it. Patients who have chemotherapy, which induces nausea, will afterwards avoid whatever they ate prior to the treatment session.[6]

Another example of an involuntary reflex is the situation this chapter began with, which is based on a true story.[7] The child had stuck his fingers in his ears like that on more than one occasion, and the parent scolded the child and forbade him from doing it again. It turned out the child had hyper-sensitive hearing and was experiencing genuine pain when noise levels became too intense for him. But he learnt to suppress sticking his fingers in his ears because it had been forbidden. This made it take longer to identify the underlying condition because that outward sign of it had been removed.

Some people have senses that are highly sensitive to stimuli, triggering in them a nervous system reflex in situations in which most people would not experience that and therefore most people would not expect such a reaction or understand that this is what has happened. In London on 2 June 2022 at the celebrations for Queen Elizabeth II's platinum jubilee, the British Royal Family came out onto the balcony of Buckingham Palace to wave at the enormous crowds of people and watch an aerial display of dozens of aircraft flying over the palace. At a peak of the fly-past's loud engines and roar of the cheering crowd, the youngest person on the balcony, four-year-old Prince Louis, covered his ears with his hands, squeezed his eyes tight shut, and threw his mouth wide open in what appeared to me to be a scream of anguish. None of the other 15 people on the balcony reacted that way. A photograph capturing this scene appeared widely in the media, with reports of Prince Louis's 'amusing' and 'naughty' behaviour.

Being scolded is a signal of impending rejection, and because being rejected is associated with the danger of abandonment and isolation, we fear this and will typically change our behaviour to avoid disapproval and rejection. When highly sensitive individuals learn to suppress outward signals that others do not like, it makes it harder for their real experiences and needs to be suitably responded to. After Prince Louis covered his ears, he put his thumb in his mouth – a self-soothing behaviour – and his mother stopped this by firmly patting his hand in place away from his face. This type of (well-meaning) guidance and suppression happens in ordinary families all the time.

People with high sensitivity include those who have been variously termed gifted, autistic, 'the highly sensitive person',[8] and those with extreme intelligence. Such people often display involuntary behaviours they are unconscious of – often much more subtle than sticking fingers in ears – triggered by a highly sensitive nervous system, in social situations in which others do not expect this behaviour and find it inappropriate. In such situations the conversational partner often takes it personally, ascribes a psychological motivation to it, and even uses it as a basis for rejecting the person they didn't understand.

The three states of the autonomic nervous system: safety, mobilisation, immobilisation

When we feel safe, our nervous systems are in a state that promotes health, growth, and restoration.[9] This is when the parasympathetic nervous system is activated. It is when we are in a state of safety that our Social Engagement System can operate well, meaning we can feel comfortable and enjoy socialising with others.

Feeling safe is dependent on being in a state of homeostasis.[10] Homeostasis is when our bodies are at the correct temperature, and we have enough energy to fuel our desired or required activity. Also, we feel psychologically and emotionally comfortable and at peace, easily able to give our attention to people, tasks, and activities desired by us or required of us.

Moving out of homeostasis is termed 'dysregulation'. We become dysregulated when we experience the discomfort of being too hot or cold, hungry, thirsty, or tired, or something happens that we find upsetting and we feel uncomfortable feelings like anxiety, shock, fear, pain, distress, confusion, embarrassment, or jealousy. When we become dysregulated, we need something to regulate us, meaning something that will return us to homeostasis, to feeling comfortable and at peace.

If the autonomic nervous system is not in a state of safety, then it is in a state of defence. This will happen even if there is no actual threat but when something is perceived as a threat. A person can be consciously aware of what they're perceiving as a threat, or it can be perceived at the automatic and unconscious level of neuroception.

When someone does not respond as you expect within a social interaction, appearing to reject you – for example, ignoring something you say or physically turning away from you – you detect this as a threat. Threat triggers mobilisation (the second state of the nervous system) or immobilisation (the third state of the nervous system). See Table 1.1 for a summary of the three states of the autonomic nervous system.

Mobilisation happens when nerves around the spine that form the sympathetic nervous system get activated, triggering a response of fight or flight. This causes your heart rate to accelerate, your breathing to become more rapid and shallow, and other physiological changes that prepare you for self-protective action. If this happens during a conversation and you react by saying something combative, this is the fight reaction. Walking away from the situation is the flight reaction.

Immobilisation is the freeze reaction. This involves the nervous system shutting down. This would be the response of going silent and physically still, your mind blank, or when you start thinking of something else as though you're not even there anymore. Another term for this state is 'dissociation'. A more extreme version of this is fainting. It is the defence reaction of 'playing dead'

Safety	Mobilisation	Immobilisation
Parasympathetic nervous system is activated.	Sympathetic nervous system is activated.	Shutdown of nervous system.
Social Engagement System is operating.	Fight or Flight response.	Freeze response.
Feeling relaxed, social, playful, intimate.	Feeling angry or afraid.	Collapse: becoming dissociated, fainting.

Table 1.1 The three states of the autonomic nervous system

that gets triggered when it is not an option to either fight or flee. For example, a mouse in a cat's jaws cannot fight back or flee so it goes immobile.[11]

Again, this is not a decision you make, it is a completely involuntary response. During my training to do a parachute jump the instructor told us, 'When you are up in the air and must step out of the plane, you will find that something powerful takes over that can make it impossible to jump. It's called the survival instinct'. He was right. However much I knew intellectually that it was my choice to jump, when I stood at the open door of the plane at an altitude of 3,000 metres and saw the world below me and felt the powerful rush of air from the flying plane against my face, I became immobilised – I could not move. I had to be pushed.

Because immobilisation happens when neither fight nor flight is possible, it is what occurs in reaction to the most extreme or life-threatening of dangers. In Star Trek whenever that most lethal enemy the Borg is encountered, it always says in its robotic voice, 'Resistance is futile'. It is so powerful that no fight is possible, no flight. So just freeze, and submit. The freeze response, with dissociation, is what victims of serious abuse – such as rape – tend to experience. This is often not understood, with people saying things like – but why didn't you fight back or run away?

The vagus nerve is central in these reactions, running in two branches between the brain stem and the visceral organs of the body, carrying messages in two directions, from the brain to the lungs, heart, gut, and so on and from these organs back to the brain. One branch – the ventral vagus – engages a state of safety by down-regulating the sympathetic nervous system, which is like putting a brake on fight/flight/freeze responses. The other – the dorsal vagus – triggers those responses.

The more time a person spends in a state of safety, with their parasympathetic nervous system activated, the better their overall physical and mental health will be. The more time a person spends in a state of defence, with their sympathetic nervous system activated or in a state of nervous system collapse, the more their overall health will suffer.

You can improve the tone of the ventral vagus through breathing exercises (see the boxout at the end of this chapter on 'How to breathe') and practices like meditation, yoga, and even singing – especially together with others – which strengthens the vagus nerve's capacity to down-regulate the sympathetic nervous system and keep you in the safe state.

If we have been triggered into a state of defence – with mobilisation or immobilisation – how can we get back to safety? Or in other words, when we have become dysregulated, how can we become regulated again?

Co-regulation: connecting with others for safety is a biological imperative

Co-regulation is something mammals are genetically designed to do. Co-regulation means seeking close interactions with others of the same species, because it is connecting with others in this way that produces a state of safety. For mammals, an absence of such interactions with others in itself produces dysregulation. (Even the medical world has caught onto this, replacing the prescription of drugs, where relevant, with social prescription.[12])

Our autonomic nervous system is designed to respond to visual, auditory, and tactile behaviours from others as signals of safety, or danger, at an involuntary and unconscious level – in other words, at the level of neuroception. This begins at birth.

Each of us begins life as a helpless and vulnerable baby, entirely dependent on others for our survival. We are born genetically programmed to seek relationships with others to encourage protection and care from them. Babies turn their heads to the sound of a human voice and search out eye contact, showing more interest in human faces than in any other visual stimulus.[13]

When a baby is physiologically dysregulated (hungry, tired, too hot, too cold) and also when it is emotionally dysregulated – lonely, afraid, overstimulated, bored – the baby signals this by crying. Hopefully a caregiver is at hand to attend to the cry, interpret its cause, and take steps to provide what the baby needs, whether physical (such as a blanket or food) or emotional (such as company, comfort, a soothing voice, or touch).

When a caregiver responds accurately to the cry and the baby calms, this in turn calms the caregiver, making them both feel safe. It is termed co-regulation because we do it for each other, mutually affecting each other.

If a baby's dysregulated state is not adequately responded to, it can even be fatal. Physical dysregulation is usually obvious to people. It is well known a baby will die of starvation if left hungry, or it can die of overheating if, for example, left in an unventilated car in the sun.

It is less known that emotional dysregulation also has severe consequences. This has been demonstrated in many studies on Romanian orphanages where infants were given the physical necessities for survival but beyond that were ignored – not given physical holding and stroking or individually directed one-to-one social interaction. Children raised in this way developed what is termed 'non-organic failure to thrive', which includes lack of physical growth, developmental delays, affective symptoms such as anxiety, and disruptive behaviour.[14] Those who survived developed long-term mental health conditions and showed permanent cognitive impairment.[15]

Throughout our lives, we benefit from loving physical touch and positive and meaningful one-to-one social interaction. Even positive conversations without physical contact produce in us feel-good biochemicals such as endorphins and dopamine and the bonding hormone of oxytocin, which have long-lasting effects.[16] We instinctively seek belonging with others with whom we feel safe. Isolation is associated with danger. We react with intense negative feelings (fear, pain) if we experience rejection, exclusion, hostility, abandonment, isolation.[17] If subjected to such conditions in a way that is intense, repeated, or long term, we become traumatised.

While in early life co-regulation is achieved by loving physical touch and the sound of a positive voice, by adulthood when language has developed it is not just the sound of the voice that can achieve this but also the content – the meaning of the words spoken. What you say – or write – to someone can act as a calming stroke. Or a signal of danger.

We crave positive interaction with others so much that we can adapt to receiving drastically watered-down and even meaningless approximations of this as calming signals of acceptance and safety – such as receiving likes on social media from strangers or the generic soothing sounds of ASMR (Autonomic Sensory Meridian Response) emitted by cartoons on YouTube. That is why social media can be addictive, because it feeds this craving for being noticed, accepted, liked, belonging. (And it can be equally destructive, delivering cues of exclusion and rejection through cyberbullying or even Facebook photographs of others having fun without you.)

Self-regulation

Self-regulation means the ability to detect for yourself that you are in a dys-regulated state, identify what is needed for regulation, and yourself take action to restore homeostasis. When a caregiver provides regulation over and over again, the baby internalises it. This means the growing child builds a model of what kind of thing is needed for helping with which kind of experience of dysregulation, so that later when the caregiver is not present, they can draw on this learning and know how to regulate themselves.

Here is an example. A mother says to a child, 'Look, you're shivering, how are you feeling? You must be really cold! Here, put on this warm jumper'. From this, the child learns the following five things:

1　Even if I feel distressed by this uncomfortable feeling, there is someone who is not worried about it – they are familiar with it and know what to do about it.

2   This form of uncomfortable feeling is associated with this form of physical manifestation – shivering.
3   There is a word for this experience – it is called being cold.
4   There is a remedy for this – it is to put on a warm item of clothing.
5   There is someone I can trust to help me – when I have uncomfortable feelings I can turn to someone else and this will make me feel better.

What the mother says in this example sounds incredibly basic, and yet you can see the complexity of what it achieves. In healthy households, such caregiving interactions happen automatically, repeatedly, without anyone even really thinking about it. Such regular, reliable interactions build for the child a pattern of feeling safe in relationships. It is what psychoanalyst John Bowlby called a 'secure attachment'.[18]

Where this kind of care is lacking, and depending on what pattern of care is given, the child can instead build an anxious attachment[19] (similar to a fight reaction), or an avoidant attachment[20] (similar to a flight reaction). These are both forms of insecure attachment. When there is severe neglect or abuse, a disorganised attachment is formed[21] (similar to a freeze reaction). These patterns of how we are impacted by the kind of care we predominantly receive have been demonstrated by decades of international research in Attachment Theory. Bowlby showed that the more secure a person feels, the more freely they will explore their environment.[22] This is why secure attachment is associated with higher levels of curiosity and learning.

The results of failure in care can be shocking. For example, a neglected child of primary school age is seen on the school playground, in the winter, wearing only shorts and a t-shirt, shivering and running around behaving aggressively towards other children.[23] His aggression (sympathetic nervous system mobilised, fight reaction) comes from the fact he is not feeling safe: he is feeling very uncomfortable but doesn't know why or what to do about it, because no one has taught him that what he is feeling is too cold, and no-one has provided the basic care of linking this with the need for warm clothes or given him these on a winter day.

Poor self-regulation does not always stem from failures in caregiving – it can also stem from a developmental disability, meaning that a person's neurophysiological functioning has not developed in the typical way to take on the functions of independent self-regulation. Cynthia Kim, who has a diagnosis of ASD, describes how she cannot easily identify what is causing her own dysregulation or what to do about it.[24] She explains this as arising from deficits in the area of brain functioning termed 'executive function'.[25]

Regulation – through co-regulation, and self-regulation – is one of the most important capabilities a growing human being can acquire. Weakness in or failure of regulation underlies every kind of mental health and behavioural problem. Just like the child on the playground who behaves aggressively because he cannot find a way of regaining a comfortable homeostasis for himself, all aggression towards others in adulthood derives from the perpetrator experiencing an uncomfortably dysregulated state that they cannot manage to regulate.

Even the creature that Frankenstein[26] created only became a monster because his deep suffering at being feared and rejected and his desperate pleas for someone who would accept and love him, thereby soothing him and bringing him happiness, were ignored and refused.

Without others to co-regulate with us and help develop healthy self-regulation, we will seek other methods. For example, we might turn to substances like alcohol or drugs – even food – and use these in dangerous excess in an attempt to get out of an uncomfortably dysregulated feeling state (distress, anger, loneliness, emptiness, boredom, anxiety) into a more comfortable, regulated feeling state. Self-harm such as cutting is an attempt to self-regulate. The most extreme version of this – suicide – is when a person ends the unbearable feelings by ending their life.

Emotion mind, Reason mind, Wise mind

When we become dysregulated, we might feel a strong emotion, such as fear or anger, and when we are feeling something like that, it is hard to think clearly. The part of the brain that gets activated to deal with fight or flight (the amygdala) is different from the part of the brain that gets activated when we think rationally (the prefrontal cortex). Daniel Goleman, founder of the concept of emotional intelligence, describes becoming upset as being hijacked by the amygdala.[27]

Methods of trying to avert an instant damaging response when angry, such as counting to ten before you respond, are designed to help re-engage the prefrontal cortex, because it is that part of the brain that can count, rather than the amygdala. Trying to strengthen the prefrontal cortex in such a situation helps you to think about what kind of response is best rather than just act impulsively when feeling something strong.

Marsha Linehan, founder of Dialectical Behaviour Therapy (DBT), described this in a useful way. She talked about each of us having three states of mind – Emotion mind, Reason mind, and Wise mind.[28] All three are important, but it is helpful to be able to identify which one is dominating for us at different points. If you become very angry and want to divorce your spouse, Emotion mind is dominating. At that point you just want to get away from that person and punish them and you're not thinking about the bigger picture – you're not able to think clearly while feeling something so strongly.

When Reason mind is dominant, you might be ignoring the emotional aspects of a situation. For example, you get a job offer that involves relocating to a different country. With Reason mind you just want the job for career progression and income but you're not in touch with the emotional impact on yourself and loved ones of moving away.

The most integrated way of dealing with any situation is when Wise mind is dominating, because it combines Emotion mind and Reason mind. This means you are able to think clearly about a situation while also being in touch with your feelings about the situation. Taking into account the rational aspects plus the emotional ones creates wisdom: when Wise mind is in operation you are most likely to make the best choices.

Defences: Shakespeare's snail

The defensive reactions of fight, flight, and freeze can operate in a very physically noticeable way – such as a person punching someone, or running away, or fainting – but they can also operate in more hidden psychological ways. This was first detailed in Anna Freud's 1937 book on 'mechanisms of defence'.[29] Each defence involves making a psychological manoeuvre that aims to restore a sense of safety by trying to remove something dysregulating from your awareness or trying to remove it from the awareness of someone else who you fear would disapprove. This will be explored more in the next chapters.

Defence of any kind always originates as an adaptive response – an attempt to restore safety.[30] But that defensive behaviour can then in itself become a problem. This happens when the defence becomes habitual, occurring in situations where it is inappropriate because there is no actual threat so it is not needed, and instead of being helpful, it prevents a person from engaging in behaviours and activities that are known to be positive for health, growth, and restoration. For example, experiencing trauma in a relationship can make you avoid ever getting close to anyone again, which then prevents you from deriving the benefit of co-regulation with others that promotes health, growth, and restoration. A person to whom this happens can then stay isolated within a state of defence, which in itself leads to health problems.

It is like this quote from William Shakespeare:

> . . . the snail, whose tender horns being hit,
> Shrinks backward in his shelly cave with pain,
> And there all smother'd up in shade doth sit,
> Long after fearing to creep forth again.[31]

Each of us is like Shakespeare's snail. When we engage in conversation with another person, we do so from inside our shells. If we feel safe, we can venture out of those shells, but we always do so with our tender horns out like antennae, feeling for danger, and if the tender horn is hit, back we shrink, fearful of coming out again.

The special vulnerability of those who have extreme intelligence

Extreme intelligence is an individual difference marked by three main features: a biological basis, minority status, and related physiological, experiential, and behavioural characteristics.[32]

1   *Biological basis.* Brain structure (cranial capacity, or brain size, and volume of grey matter and density of white matter) and brain function (neural efficiency) are much greater than the norm.[33]

2   *Minority status.* This neurodivergence is found in fewer than 2% of people in a general population.
3   *Related physiological, experiential, and behavioural characteristics.* These combined facts of atypical brain biology and minority status pervasively affect how such a person experiences the world and behaves, because their cognitive functioning and general physiological sensitivity are much higher than the neurotypical majority of the population.

Being in a minority means such a person is often not understood, leading to regular experiences of their 'tender horns' being hit over and over again in interactions with others. This even begins with caregivers.

When a parent doesn't understand a child's extremely sensitive responses to its environment, these can look to the parent like *over*-reactions. Like in the example of the child sticking his fingers in his ears, the parent didn't understand what the child was experiencing that caused that behaviour, so instead of helping to regulate the child's difficult feelings, the parent scolded him. If the child does not comply, he might be judged as badly behaved. What such a child internalises is that someone else can't help, someone else will be angry with me, so I must hide what I'm feeling.

When a parent cannot calm their child, the child remains distressed, but also the parent feels bad – in other words, co-regulation fails. Such failures threaten bonding, which is the building of a relationship in which you are in synchrony with each other and naturally seek more interactions with each other because they make (both of) you feel good.

When such a child goes to school, they encounter the effects of educational systems that are unsuitable for them because they are designed to cater to the majority. This means that the activities they are meant to spend all day on will lead to dysregulation for them – boredom, frustration – which can manifest in behavioural problems.

I've described how we search for a sense of belonging with others as a way of feeling safe. One way that we assess whether we belong with someone is by searching for signs of similarity between ourselves. We look into another person's face to find whether the expression we see there mirrors what we are feeling. Are your reactions to things similar to the reactions I'm having? When feelings and reactions are mirrored between people, this establishes a sense of understanding between them, and safety. It's what psychoanalyst Heinz Kohut called a 'twinship transference'[34] – that experience of joy at realising 'you're just like me!' The one thing begged for by the creature Frankenstein made was that Frankenstein would make another being as a companion for him who would be the same kind of creature as himself.

When an interaction with someone goes well, and we feel accepted, that feels good and builds our self-esteem. There is a natural wish to want more of what feels good. If we have repeated interactions with someone that go well, we start to build with that person a comfort zone. We naturally gravitate towards social situations that are within our comfort zone.

In conversations where an extremely intelligent person's mind is working far ahead of where the other person is at, or at a greater level of complexity than the other person is engaging with, and they speak faster than the other person can keep up with, there can be many awkward or unpleasant moments that trip up the Social Engagement System, triggering states of defence rather than states of safety.

Individuals with extreme intelligence can also unwittingly trigger defences in others. Just being the way they are often causes hits to the 'tender horns' of others. One of the reasons for this is that people often experience high intelligence as a threat[35] – they can be caused to feel a sense of personal inadequacy when they observe in someone else a greater proficiency than their own, which can make them feel bad about themselves and uncomfortable with that person. They could therefore prefer to avoid that person. This often happens to an extremely intelligent child during their early experiences at school.

Here is an example of how this can play out. At school, six-year-old Ana has advanced intellectual development that makes reading very easy for her. On the playground she tries to play with her peers but experiences that this doesn't go well – the other children don't seem to be on the same wavelength as she is and they respond in a way that is rejecting or even bullying. This provokes intense negative feelings (dysregulation) in Ana that she wants to get rid of. She finds that reading a book distracts her from these unhappy experiences. Reading is performing a function for her of self-regulation.

Ana learns that reading is a much safer and more enjoyable activity than trying to interact with her peers. She begins to avoid going out onto the playground, instead taking refuge in the school library. She develops a pattern of suppressing difficult feelings by turning instead to thinking and reading. Through practising this repeatedly, she becomes more and more intellectually advanced and less and less practised at and comfortable with interacting with peers socially.

This story describes the development of the psychological defence of intellectualisation and its repercussions. As Ana grows up, this defence becomes the safe place in her mind, as though she is carrying the refuge of the library around with her. In this defence the left hemisphere of the brain with its reliance on words, reason, and logic shuts out and becomes more and more disconnected from the right hemisphere of the brain with its images, intuitions, feelings.

At the age of 36, Ana is single, a virgin, lives alone. She is successful in her career but often changes jobs because she falls out with others at work, feeling they don't understand her and exclude her. In therapy sessions with me, I find it hard to reach her emotionally because she has become very dissociated from her feelings. When any difficult feelings come up, she quickly switches to intellectualisation, protecting herself with clever words, trying to spar with me, pick at my words. I struggle to find a way to like her. The only way I can relate to her is by remembering that there is a tender, afraid, wounded self who is hidden very deep inside her shell.

Unfortunately, this is a not uncommon pattern in children who have extreme intelligence.

All of this can lead to a person who has extreme intelligence becoming isolated, experiencing themselves as outsiders. In my psychotherapy practice I see over and over again how much the experience of not fitting in, and not belonging, has created deep wounds for very high-IQ people. It is something I have clients talking about regularly, weeping about, describing as the one thing that most deeply distresses them, that feeling of not being accepted, being different, and sensing that while your abilities might be valued and respected, you are not liked, you are not invited to join in. Not being invited to join in is a repeated theme, and how much it hurts. There remains the deep longing to find similarity and belonging – and safety – in relationships with others. When they find this, the joy it brings is immense. But with that, there is a process of learning and adaptation they need to go through to relinquish old defences that are no longer serving them and are impeding them, and move from a state of defence to a state of safety with its greater freedom to explore, be curious, learn, and enjoy.

Ways of relating with others[36]

I see the way we relate to others as being primarily affected by a combination of how freely we are able to express ourselves and how much acceptance we experience from others. I created a framework that demonstrates this – see Figure 1.1.

In this framework, how we express ourselves (the horizontal line) and what level of acceptance we receive from others (the vertical line) intersect to produce four quadrants. The two quadrants on the left, labelled 'Hiding Self', involve a person withdrawing from expressing themselves, like Shakespeare's snail hiding in its shell.

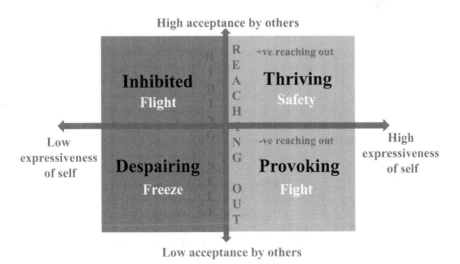

Figure 1.1 Ways of relating with others

The bottom-left quadrant, 'Despairing', happens when a person's expressiveness has led to traumatic experiences of rejection like bullying and abuse. They are caught predominantly in the 'freeze' state, in which they are often dissociated, and they avoid close relationships with others. The top-left quadrant, 'Inhibited', is when a person is not in a state of trauma but has withdrawn from expressing themselves. They are interpersonally predominantly in a state of 'flight'.

The two quadrants on the right, labelled 'Reaching Out', show a person being able to be more self-expressive, reaching out to others but in ways that can be positive (top-right quadrant, labelled 'Thriving') or negative (bottom-right quadrant, labelled 'Provoking'). In the 'Provoking' quadrant, a person is angry, existing predominantly in a 'fight' state in relation to others. In the 'Thriving' quadrant, a person is predominantly in a state of safety, feeling a freedom to reach out self-expressively to others in a way that is positive, and experiencing high levels of acceptance from others.

You might experience yourself relating to others in ways that fit within different quadrants at different times, but you will mostly be located within one of the quadrants in the way you relate to others. It is optimal to be located in the 'Thriving' quadrant. My work with my psychotherapy clients is about helping them to move into this quadrant. The communication skills presented in the rest of the book are designed to assist readers to express themselves more freely in a way that can receive high levels of acceptance from others, to catalyse movement into the 'Thriving' quadrant. The more time we spend in the 'Thriving' quadrant, in a state of safety, the better our relationships, occupational performance, and overall health will be.

Do try this at home – Chapter 1 boxout

This is a simple breathing exercise in three steps that is research-evidenced to aid self-regulation, meaning it will help calm down a nervous system that is jumping to a state of defence. Breathing like this will reduce anxiety and increase focus. Once you have become familiar with the method, it is easy and fully portable: you can use it anywhere, anytime. Whenever anything at all makes you feel uncomfortable, make breathing like this the first thing you do.

How to breathe

1. **Rest a hand at the base of your ribs.** This is where your diaphragm is. (This method is called 'diaphragmatic breathing', or 'belly breathing'.)
2. **Place of breathing: Breathe in through your nose, sending the breath towards that hand – feel how the in-breath makes**

your body push against your hand as your lungs fill with air – then breathe out through your nose. This ensures you are breathing in the most beneficial way, which is deeply, lower down towards your abdomen, rather than shallowly, higher up towards your chest and neck. When you first try this, you might find it helps to lie on your back to relax your body and pay attention to how your breathing moves the hand that's resting at the base of your ribs. Once you are familiar with how to breathe correctly into your diaphragm, it's not something you have to lie down for, and you can do it any time and any place. It's helpful to check on your breathing during the day – simply notice whether your chest is rising and falling (shallow breathing) or whether your stomach is rising and falling (deep breathing), and adjust from shallow to deeper breathing. Ensure your breath is going to the right place in your body before you move to the next step.

3. **Pace of breathing: Breathe in to a count of three, and then breathe out to a count of seven. Repeat several times.** You can adjust the number of counts per breath according to what works best for you, as long as you always follow this rule: the out-breath must last for more counts than the in-breath. Another way you can do this is to breathe in for a few counts, hold your breath for a few counts, then breathe out for a few counts (and you can even hold for a few counts again before the next in-breath). Experiment to find what the pattern is that follows the rule and feels most comfortable for you and easy to remember.

This place and pace of breathing counteracts anxiety because it is the opposite of how our bodies automatically begin breathing when going into fight or flight. It counteracts hyperventilation, which is what produces panic attacks. Commit this pattern of breathing to memory and regularly practice it. When it has become second nature, you won't even have to put your hand in place but can skip straight to step 3.

Notes

1 My understanding of the neurophysiology involved here is informed primarily by the work of Stephen Porges and his Polyvagal Theory.
2 Porges (2017).
3 Porges (2017).
4 Porges (2017).
5 Porges (2017).
6 Porges (2017).
7 A case mentioned in Porges (2017).
8 Aron (1999).
9 Porges (2017).

10 Porges (2017).
11 Porges (2017).
12 For example, see Morton et al. (2015).
13 See Libertus et al. (2017).
14 For example, see Ellis et al. (2004).
15 Sonuga-Barke et al. (2017).
16 See Glaser and Glaser (2014).
17 See discussion and references in Falck (2020, p. 54).
18 Bowlby (1969, 1988).
19 Ainsworth et al. (1978).
20 Ainsworth et al. (1978).
21 Main and Solomon (1986).
22 Bowlby (1969, 1988).
23 True case example given by children's charity Place2Be.
24 Kim (2015).
25 A resource for reading about executive function is Honos-Webb (2018).
26 Shelley (1818).
27 Goleman (1996).
28 See Linehan (2015).
29 Freud (1937).
30 Porges (2017).
31 Shakespeare (1593/2007).
32 See Falck (2020), particularly pp. 56–59.
33 See Haier (2017) and other sources summarised in Falck (2020).
34 Kohut (1971).
35 In the section on 'Our Fear of Intelligence', in Falck (2021, pp. 18–20), I explained the different ways that people can experience high intelligence as a threat.
36 For an in-depth explanation of this framework, see the chapter in my first book titled 'Hiding Self, Reaching Out' (Falck, 2020, Chapter 8, pp. 154–172). The version shown in the current book is a simplification of my original framework and adds the fight/flight/freeze designations.

References

Ainsworth, M.D., Blehar, M.C., Waters, E. and Wall, S. (1978). *Patterns of Attachment: A Psychological Study of the Strange Situation*. Hillsdale, NJ: Erlbaum.

Aron, E.N. (1999). *The Highly Sensitive Person*. London: HarperCollins Publishers.

Bowlby, J. (1969). *Attachment and Loss: Vol. 1, Attachment*. New York: Basic Books.

Bowlby, J. (1988). *A Secure Base*. London: Routledge.

Ellis, B.H., Fisher, P.A. and Zaharie, S. (2004). Predictors of Disruptive Behavior, Developmental Delays, Anxiety, and Affective Symptomatology among Institutionally Reared Romanian Children. *Journal of the American Academy of Child & Adolescent Psychiatry*, 43(10), pp. 1283–1292. doi:10.1097/01.chi.0000136562.24085.160.

Falck, S. (2020). *Extreme Intelligence – Development, Predicaments, Implications*. London: Routledge.

Falck, S. (2021). *The Psychology of Intelligence*. London: Routledge.

Freud, A. (1937). *The Ego and the Mechanisms of Defence* (Revised ed., 2018). New York: Routledge.

Glaser, J.E. and Glaser, R.D. (2014). The Neurochemistry of Positive Conversations. [online] *Harvard Business Review*. Available at: https://hbr.org/2014/06/the-neurochemistry-of-positive-conversations [Accessed 16 July 2022].

Goleman, D. (1996). *Emotional Intelligence: Why It Can Matter More Than IQ*. London: Bloomsbury.

Haier, R.J. (2017). *The Neuroscience of Intelligence*. Cambridge: Cambridge University Press.

Honos-Webb, L. (2018). *Brain Hacks*. Emeryville, CA: Althea Press.

Kim, C. (2015). *Nerdy, Shy, and Socially Inappropriate*. London: Jessica Kingsley Publishers.

Kohut, H. (1971). *The Analysis of the Self* (Reprint 2009). Chicago, IL: University of Chicago Press.

Libertus, K., Landa, R.J. and Haworth, J.L. (2017). Development of Attention to Faces during the First 3 Years: Influences of Stimulus Type. *Frontiers in Psychology*, 8. doi:10.3389/fpsyg.2017.01976.

Linehan, M.M. (2015). *DBT Skills Training Manual* (2nd ed.). New York: The Guilford Press.

Main, M. and Solomon, J. (1986). Discovery of an Insecure-disorganized/Disoriented Attachment Pattern. In T.B. Brazelton and M.W. Yogman (eds) *Affective Development in Infancy*. Norwood, NJ: Ablex Publishing Corporation, pp. 95–124.

Morton, L., Ferguson, M. and Baty, F. (2015). Improving wellbeing and self-efficacy by social prescription. *Portal Komunikacii Naukowej*, 129(3), pp. 286–289.

Porges, S.W. (2017). *The Pocket Guide to the Polyvagal Theory: The Transformative Power of Feeling Safe*. New York: W.W. Norton & Company.

Shakespeare, W. (1593/2007). Venus & Adonis. In D. Bevington and D.S. Kastan (eds) *William Shakespeare: The Poems*. New York: Bantam Books.

Shelley, M. (1818). *Frankenstein* (Reprinted 2018). New York: Penguin Books.

Sonuga-Barke, E.J.S., Kennedy, M., Kumsta, R., Knights, N., Golm, D., Rutter, M., Maughan, B., Schlotz, W. and Kreppner, J. (2017). Child-to-Adult Neurodevelopmental and Mental Health Trajectories after Early Life Deprivation: The Young Adult Follow-up of the Longitudinal English and Romanian Adoptees Study. *The Lancet*, [online] 389(10078), pp. 1539–1548. doi:10.1016/s0140-6736(17)30045-4.

2   The barrister's case

When two people talk, each affects the other and the way the conversation unfolds in ways they are only partially aware of. Some of what goes on between them will only be noticed if the conversation is reflected on afterwards. To demonstrate a case of this, and as a way of introducing some typical complications that can arise and trip up conversations with someone who has extreme intelligence, I will share and discuss in detail a conversation I had with a member of the international high-IQ society Mensa.[1]

The conversation came about because as part of my doctoral research I interviewed adults with giftedness/very high IQ/extreme intelligence. This is true of all members of Mensa because the only requirement for gaining membership is evidence of having taken a standardised IQ test on which you obtained a score higher than that of at least 98% of the general population. Mensa also run their own supervised IQ tests which anyone can book a place on, and if you gain this eligible score Mensa will invite you to join.

Mensa was founded by two barristers in 1946, and the conversation I discuss in this chapter is one I had with a barrister – I'll call him Mr. B. The conversation took place at my consulting room in Harley Street. What I present here are the actual words that were spoken between us, copied from the transcript of the audio-recorded interview (page numbers from the transcript are included). For ease of distinguishing who is speaking, I have put all of Mr. B's speech in italics. Throughout, dotted lines appear where content has been omitted to preserve anonymity.

What do you say about yourself when you meet someone?

At the beginning of the interview, I knew nothing about Mr. B other than that he was a Mensa member who had volunteered to meet with me for this research interview. So I opened the interview by saying:

ME: (p. 1) Well if I can start by just getting a few details about your background of where you grew up, your education, qualifications, and so on.

DOI:10.4324/9781003029106-4

He responded by stating where he grew up and then said this:

MR. B: *I've got a bachelor's degree in . . . , I've got another bachelor's degree in . . . , I've got a master's degree in . . . and one more master's degree in. . . . And I'm currently working towards a PhD. In between I've also been trained in . . . law, . . . law, also in . . . law, . . . law. That's about it.*

I found it striking that he chose to give that level of detail of his achievements. He could have simply said he had studied law and was now qualified as a barrister. Perhaps he thought I wanted that level of detail. But this itemised list of achievements is even more striking when contrasted with something from later in the interview, when he said:

MR. B: *(p. 29) I would never go out of my way to tell people that I've got so many degrees or I do this or I'm an expert in that . . .*

It could be said he did go out of his way to tell me he has so many degrees, because he responded to an interview advert, made the effort to come and meet me, and when asked about his background, immediately went into such detail. It makes me think of a child who paints a picture and very naturally wants to show it to someone, wanting acknowledgement for what they've achieved. But a child with extreme intelligence, who often achieves better results than others around them, is soon told not to draw attention to what they've done. Being good at something instantly switches any seeking of acknowledgement of it to being seen as boasting, showing off, which is almost universally disapproved of.[2] Mr. B himself disapproves of this:

MR. B: *(p. 20) Blowing your own horn kind of a thing is not something that's very nice, and in fact if somebody were to come to me and say, 'You know I do this a lot and I'm extremely good at this and I'm extremely good at that', I would not rate that person very high.*

And yet, it is a basic human need to want to be noticed and acknowledged and accepted for who you are and what you have done. The quote continued like this:

MR. B: *(p. 29) I would never go out of my way to tell people that I've got so many degrees or I do this or I'm an expert in that. But if somebody found out something about me, that would give me a huge amount of happiness.*

So, Mr. B has the dilemma that he would love to have the happiness of acknowledgement from others, but there is a cultural prohibition against straightforwardly seeking this. What is he to do?

MR. B: *(p. 29) It's much more satisfying if people discover who you are and come back to you and say, 'My God I didn't know this about you', rather than you're having to tell them, 'I am fantastic, I'm very good at what I do.'*

Mr. B's solution to the dilemma seems to be to deny there is anything special about him in a way that provokes someone else to say it for him. Someone like me. It was only after the interview, when analysing it, that I noticed a repeating sequence between us where he would deny he had any special capabilities, I would say but what about this or that accomplishment (facts I could only refer to because he had already provided me with them), and then he would again be dismissive of them.

ME: (p. 3) So the advert you responded to used the word 'gifted' and I wonder how you feel that relates to you?

MR. B: *I don't feel that applies at all to me, I don't, no.*

. . .

ME: (p. 6) [You said] you don't see yourself as intellectually gifted. You've obviously succeeded very well, lots of high-level degrees, been successful in your career?

MR. B: *I don't know if I've been successful.*

. . .

ME: (p. 7) So the fact that you achieved [I mention an accomplishment he told me of that is unique within his field], how did that come about if it doesn't really mean anything?

MR. B: *Luck I think, just right place right time.*

. . .

MR. B: *(p. 24) Extremely lucky. I call it luck.*

ME: Yes I hear that. You don't give yourself any credit for . . .

MR. B: *Anybody could have done what I've done. I've done nothing special.*

It is patently obvious not everybody could have done all Mr. B has achieved. Trying to deny this, or pretending not to care about it, contradicts the fact that he voluntarily sought Mensa membership and voluntarily responded to an advert that asked for 'gifted adults'. Contradictions, pretence, and false modesty can make a conversational partner feel uneasy and unsure of whether they can trust you, rather than promoting the state of safety that enables good social connection.

Mr. B's inner conflict about this aspect of himself – his extreme intelligence – reflects a conflict in our wider culture around intelligence. In general, being called intelligent is a compliment, and being called stupid is an insult. But being 'too' intelligent is scorned – 'clever clogs', 'smart arse', 'know-it-all'. So there is a mixed message about whether intelligence is prized or scorned, and whether high achievement should be strived for and celebrated or avoided and hidden away as though it is something shameful.[3] Someone with identified extreme intelligence can therefore experience it as a 'stigmatised identity'[4] – meaning an identity that attracts social discrimination – and struggle with how to manage this in social situations. Mr. B's evident struggle with this is the same quandary anyone experiences who has a stigmatised identity: do they reveal it, or, where possible, should they rather keep it concealed?

At one point Mr. B admitted, 'I do know that I've succeeded a little more than my peers' (p. 6). But mostly he seemed at pains to portray himself as no different from anyone else. Excelling beyond others, being an outlier, sets you apart from others, and this can be a lonely place.

How do you find others with whom you can belong?

MR. B: *(p. 3) It feels nice to be a part of a society of . . . you know which is very exclusive. So I applied to Mensa, I was tested. They said, 'Welcome aboard', so I joined up.*

Seeking membership of a society grouped around a named individual difference – in this case extreme intelligence – is a way of seeking belonging with others who share this similarity with yourself. But if the individual difference involved is a stigmatised identity, a person's wish to belong can be countered by mixed feelings about whether they want to admit they are 'one of them'. So while Mr. B said it 'feels nice' to be part of Mensa, he also said (p. 3), *'I haven't participated in any Mensa activities or anything'*. Nearly all the Mensa members I have encountered have told me they choose not to disclose that they have this membership.

Mr. B went on to say:

MR. B: *(p. 3–4) I'm not very happy meeting people, I'm what you would call an introvert. . . . In fact I'm happier talking to people over the telephone or over the internet than I am in person.*

ME: Well I'm surprised you came here then. You had the option of Skype. It's very nice that you came.

MR. B: *No there's a very, very good answer for that and that is as far as I'm concerned, this is our only meeting. Even if you judge me it doesn't matter. You are a stranger, I'm probably never going to run into you again, so it doesn't matter.*

ME: So if there was a possibility of meeting again, you'd have preferred doing it by internet?

MR. B: *I would have thought very long and hard about whether I would do it in the first place or not.*

ME: Oh I see, okay.

MR. B: *Because most of the time we do put on an act don't we, everybody does? . . . So it's too much of an effort.*

ME: I see. So I'm going to get the act for an hour and a half?

MR. B: *Not really, no.*

. . .

ME: (p. 5) And so what made you decide to answer this advert?

MR. B: *Well too much spare time, I think. I was getting bored, and this came along and I thought, 'Well why not?'*

ME: Okay, well I'm glad you did.

Here it seems I picked up on the vulnerability involved for him of talking with someone else – me, a stranger to him – and his expectation that I might 'judge' him, because I responded by reassuring him, saying, 'It's very nice that you came', and 'I'm glad you did'. I was letting him know I wanted him to be there with me, I was interested in him, and I accepted him.

It might have been this reassurance I gave him, together with the concern I showed that he might simply put on an act, that encouraged him to be more honest with me. He said:

MR. B: *(p. 5) I think talking like this helps you understand yourself a little better, so that's the real motivation. When I say too much spare time that's not possibly the honest answer. The honest answer is probably trying to discover a little bit more about myself.*

How do you try to feel comfortable with yourself in the presence of someone else?

In the foregoing sequence I was generous towards Mr. B and then he became more honest, which looks like we were creating an increasingly positive conversational climate between us. Yet soon something less comfortable appeared. He said with regard to his accomplishments:

MR. B: *(p. 7) Those are just labels. For a doctor to say I work from Harley Street, for a lawyer to say I work from Chancery Lane, it's just a label. It doesn't reflect on how well you're doing or how good you are at what you do, it's just a label isn't it?*

What he is saying makes sense. But another layer can be seen when considering that we were sitting talking inside my Harley Street consulting room, and here he was suggesting that someone working from Harley Street might not be good at what they do. This could be read as a subtle undermining of me, producing a prickle of discomfort for me. Why might he have said something to undermine me?

Up until this point in the conversation Mr. B had said he did not see himself as gifted, but when I showed I believed him, he revised it:

ME: (pp. 7–8) Okay. So you don't feel that there's something about you that you were born with that in some way makes you different from others?

MR. B: *There is definitely. I think I have a more logical mind. I can analyse much better than most people. . . . I can look at a thing and discern patterns, so I can make more sense of things. I can see things sooner than others can see the same thing given the same inputs.*

I asked him:

ME: (p. 17) . . . on a scale of one to ten, how important a part of your personal identity do you feel this is, this kind of ability to . . .

MR. B: *Ten.*

ME: Okay.

MR. B: *Absolutely.*

ME: Okay.

MR. B: *This is what defines me. If I, I have two big fears in life, as far as I am concerned, personally about myself. One is I lose my eyesight, and the second is I lose
my logical way of thinking. For me both are as good as dying. If I couldn't see
anymore I wouldn't know what to do with myself. If I didn't have my thinking, if
I could not think things through or try to understand what's going on around me,
there would be no point in living anymore would there? So a ten.*

When an identity of having high ability has become crucial to a person's sense
of self-worth, they will need to preserve that identity. And because concepts of
level of intelligence or achievement are relative – they're measured in compari-
son to others – a person to whom this has become important might form a habit
of comparing themselves with others, to reassure themselves they are maintaining their status by doing better than others. They could do this by emphasising
their own achievements but also by undermining what others have done.

MR. B: *(p. 16) I don't do a lot of things but I'm extremely good at what I do. I can't
be bothered to work very hard. . . . I'll give you an example. . . . I was invited to
an international conference where they had something like 500 [specialists] coming
from all over the world to [location] . . . and I was . . . going to be a keynote speaker
. . . I knew about two months in advance that I'm going, so I had two months
to prepare a presentation and a paper. I didn't do that. I go [there] and there was
another friend with me. . . . He was not a speaker, he just had to put up a poster or
something trivial, but he was good company, and he asked me when I landed . . .
whether I had my presentation. I said, 'I'll get around to it'. I finally got around
to starting to work on my presentation and my paper at about 1.30 at night and
I had to do it all on stage in the morning at about 10.00. So I started working
at 1.30 at night, by about 3.00 I was finished, my friend was panicking. I knew
I could do it. I knew there wasn't really a big problem and I stood up before 500
[specialists], amazingly wonderful people from all over the world, did my presentation and most of the people were extremely delighted with it. . . . I thought it was
extremely successful.*

. . .

(p. 17) I've never been a very, very hardworking person.

Here Mr. B portrays himself as someone who achieves great things effort-
lessly. He might well have a capacity to produce important work with ease
and speed. Individuals with extreme intelligence can develop a style of leaving
things to the last minute as this creates the adrenalin needed to motivate their
performance, because the task at hand is often too easy for them unless they
have added to it the challenge of a time constraint. But in what Mr. B says
above he further secures this identity of brilliance by contrasting himself with
someone else: what his friend had to do was 'trivial' compared with what he

had to do, and his friend was 'panicking', whereas he was calm – *'I knew I could do it'*.

Putting himself 'on top' of another person like this might have become a habitual way in which Mr. B tries to make himself feel comfortable, but how will these behaviours make the other person feel about him? Another problem with trying to stay on top is that you are always at risk of falling down.

What if someone discovers the 'real' you?

Straight after Mr. B first acknowledged in this conversation that he had noticed ways in which his functioning can be superior to that of others, he took an unexpected turn:

MR. B: *(p. 8) I am quite aware that most of what I do is absolutely fraud.*
ME: Fraud?
MR. B: *Yes, absolutely. There is, I was reading something about this, there's a phenomenon isn't there, where a person keeps questioning himself and saying have I deserved this or am I just faking it?*
ME: Imposter syndrome?
MR. B: *Precisely. So I have a massive dose of that.*
ME: Okay. Right. Yes I can hear that because you're talking about not really seeing yourself as in any way . . .
MR. B: *And I will not admit that to any person who I thought I would be coming into contact with again ever.*
ME: Okay, you mean that you have imposter syndrome?
MR. B: *Yeah exactly. Why would I expose myself to anybody else?*

If a person with extreme intelligence has experienced it is not easy to find others with whom they can belong and enjoy relaxed conversation in which they feel safe and accepted, they often come to prefer situations in which they have the safety of a defined role in relation to others which they are comfortable playing. Mr. B described exactly this:

MR. B: *(p. 21) I used to teach . . ., so I enjoy talking in public because it's very impersonal. When you're addressing a class you're not addressing a single person, you're putting on an act really, so I enjoy that. So going before a judge and having your wig and your gown on it's absolutely fantastic.*

Situations where there are no prescribed roles – such as unstructured socialising situations – can feel harder to navigate and these might be avoided:

ME: (p. 27) Is there something that you find difficult, the thing you find most difficult with other people at work?
MR. B: *. . . I enjoy being by myself, and it's not just at work, it's in any given situation, because there's that mask that you have to wear. . . . If at lunch time a couple*

*of my colleagues say, 'We're going across to [place] for lunch, would you like to join
us?' I would try to find an excuse to say no. Not because I don't enjoy being with
them – it's too much of an effort.*

ME: Okay, because you have the feeling that you have to put on a mask?
MR B: *Absolutely.*
ME: What do you think would happen if you didn't put on such a mask?
MR. B: *I wouldn't be happy. It's not about them, it's about me.*
ME: Okay.
MR. B: *They might discover who I am.*
ME: And do you think that would be terrible?
MR. B: *I don't know. I don't want to know.*
ME: It sounds like you fear that.
MR. B: *Possibly.*

How do you make someone feel comfortable and free in a conversation with you, or uncomfortable and restricted in what they say?

After Mr. B talked about being a fraud, he said:

MR. B: *(p. 9) I'm not making any sense, am I?*
ME: No you are, yeah.
MR. B: *Well not to myself, I'm not making any sense to myself.*
ME: Okay. Yeah, no that does make sense.

Here it seems I was again reassuring him, to make him feel more comfortable.
But perhaps there was another layer – maybe I was defending myself against
being undermined by him. Given his prior suggestion that someone who
works in Harley Street, as I did, might not be good at what they do, maybe
I was trying to show him that I was after all a competent psychotherapist –
I got his paradoxes, and I could understand things about him that he himself
didn't understand.

In my response to what Mr. B said about imposter syndrome, I continued to
be generous to him, validating his competence:

ME: (p. 10) But that probably makes you precisely better at what you do because
you're not taking it for granted that you're already okay so you keep working to make sure you haven't missed something.
MR. B: *Absolutely, all the time, but when I come across people who are extremely
successful from a worldly perspective, and who I know are absolute idiots – I am
fond of just calling people idiots, not to their face but I do feel like that. And
it's amazing. They are superbly confident, they stand up and they consider that
they're entitled to everything that they are getting and they're not really because
they are idiots.*

My validation of Mr. B seemed to make him feel comfortable enough to again be more honest and admit how he feels about other people. When he called people idiots, what would make him feel even more comfortable with me would be if I showed similarity, such as by saying I understood or felt the same way. But what he said gave me another prickle of discomfort, so I didn't respond to it. I focused on something else. Not responding to something, changing the subject, and looking away from someone are all signs of discomfort. I said:

ME: (p. 10) Okay. So this capacity you have noticed in yourself of being able to see patterns or be more logical, see things more quickly than other people can, is that something that manifested itself when you were growing up?

MR. B: . . . *There's no single point in time when I thought that this thing is manifest-ing itself, it's just that there would have been a time when I realised that something I was taking for granted was not so commonplace.*

ME: Okay, and how did you notice that?

MR. B: *Because people are idiots and they can't see what's in front of them. You have to spell it out for them.*

He appears not to have picked up on my discomfort because here he reiterated calling people idiots. And this time it made me even more uncomfortable. Not only because this was unkind and derogatory to other people but also because I knew that if he thinks this of others, he could be thinking it of me. By the very nature of the interview situation, with my questions I was causing him to have to spell things out for me. So I could feel especially at risk of being judged by him as an idiot who 'can't see what's in front of them'. It seems that this impacted me by changing the way I questioned him. I wanted to ask him what school had been like for him. I said this:

ME: (p. 18) During school were you bored? Did you find school boring or did you find it all right?

This is not a good interview question – or even a good conversational ques-tion – because it is not what is called an open question. An open question gives a person the freedom to give any kind of answer. An open question would have been, 'As a child, what was your experience of school?'

Instead, I had asked him a closed question, of the leading kind, showing that I expected he would have been bored at school. He had set up that expectation in me by all he said about his effortless achievement at the conference. But it's as though I became afraid I would look stupid if I asked a genuinely open question, so I self-protectively showed him that I was clever enough to already know the answer.

He was maybe not so much replying to my question, then, as complying with my expectation, when he responded:

MR. B: *Yes, absolutely boring.*

Maybe that was the true answer. But maybe he gave that answer because my closed question made him feel the pressure of my expectation. He might then have been protecting himself from looking stupid by not telling me anything except that school was indeed very easy for him.

The more a conversation goes in this kind of direction – threats of being judged, self-protection, closed questions, setting up expectations and complying with expectations – the more restricted and deadened it becomes. Conversation has vitality and is satisfying to the extent that the participants feel safe to freely ask open questions, give candid answers, and enjoyably adventure together into exploring fresh territory. As Bowlby said (see the previous chapter), the more secure a person feels, the more able they are to show curiosity, learn, and explore. Without that kind of spontaneity and authenticity, conversation can be reduced to a stultifying and meaningless display and a person might well choose – as Mr. B does – to stay away from it.

What happens if you keep failing to notice that you're making the other person feel uncomfortable?

If this conversation with Mr. B had been taking place in a social situation, the discomfort he was stirring in me might have prodded me to say something challenging to him (fight), find a reason to leave (flight), or shut down and dissociate from him (freeze). But because I was holding the conversation for research purposes, I did none of these things and continued engaging with him. But how might other people respond to him? The way he was behaving with me would very likely be how he also behaved with others.

I asked him how people tended to react to him:

MR. B: *(p. 11) I am labelled odd, or difficult, or awkward by most of my friends.*

ME: Are you?

MR. B: *I've got very few friends and they're extremely good friends, and they understand me, I think. But for the most part I do have a reputation of being very awkward or very odd, and I enjoy that.*

ME: Okay, so do you feel you've tried to be that, live up to that reputation?

MR. B: *I don't try at all. I think I try to be extremely nice, it's just the way things happen and I've started enjoying it.*

ME: Can you give an example of what somebody, what it might be that happens that somebody would find difficult or odd?

MR. B: *I don't know. If I knew why people found me odd I would probably try to cover that up as well. I have no idea, but that's generally the impression everybody has.*
   . . .

ME: (p. 13) Okay. Because on [the] one hand it sounds like you don't much care what people think, you can do without them, although you've also said if you knew what it was you'd probably cover it up, so that's interesting.

MR. B: *I would cover it up, not because I need those friends or because I want company, but it's always nice to have people thinking nice things about you. It's nice to be part of a group, yes, but it's. . . . It's nice to have friends but it's not so critical after all. . . . But it's nice to belong to a larger fraternity or a community or a group. It's a nice warm feeling because once you are a part of a group then you don't have to try so hard to – to get them to like you is not the correct phrase. To fit in. Then you don't have to try so hard to fit in because you're already part of it, so it's more convenient. So it's convenience rather than anything else. It's nice to be part of a group but it's not critical, it's not essential.*

He was portraying himself as self-sufficient, not really needing anyone, even enjoying being odd and different. But the other message was that if he knew what people were seeing as odd about him, he would try to cover it up. He seemed to be battling with an internal conflict around this issue: in the previous quotation he mentioned no less than six times that being part of a group was/would be 'nice' and denied three times that it had any importance for him.

Towards the end of the interview he spelled out just how painful it was for him to feel he does not fit in:

MR. B: *(p. 32) So if you were to ask somebody about me – whenever you're talking about a person you don't remember their entire personality – there would be two or three highlights that you remember and then you build your whole impression around that. That's the skeleton that you flesh out later. So the skeleton that they would have in mind is, 'Well he's not like us, he's an outsider'. I hate being an outsider, but I can't help it, I'm always an outsider. . . . Absolutely everywhere I'm an outsider. 'He's an outsider, he's not like us . . .'*

It was clear Mr. B hated being an outsider but had no awareness of how he could be contributing to this, in little ways making people feel uncomfortable with him. Could he learn how to improve this situation?

How open are you to learning new things?

Near the end of the interview I asked Mr. B, if he were to be offered coaching to do with 'how you get on with others', what would he wish it to target for him – 'What would you see as being useful?' (p. 34). He replied:

MR. B: *(p. 34) I wouldn't be very happy with that for the simple reason it would be just evidence of the fact that I'm incompetent in the first place, that somebody feels that I'm so incompetent that I need help. . . . The only way I would be comfortable with that would be if a person was smart enough to say, 'This is what needs to be done, this is what you need to learn, these are the tools, these are the resources, get on with it'. I wouldn't want somebody holding my hand or looking over my shoulder.*

Here he showed how invested he was in seeing himself as competent. He would experience a suggestion that he might be able to improve on something as an injury to his self-image. This shows a 'fixed mindset',[5] where preserving an identity of being competent is more important to a person than learning and developing further. Mr. B also expressed that if there was to be any learning, he would want to do it on his own – *'I wouldn't want somebody holding my hand or looking over my shoulder'* – presumably so that when he was next in company, he could present himself as already competent.

By contrast, a 'growth mindset' would entail having no investment in viewing or portraying oneself as already being competent. Within a growth mindset, the process of learning and discovery – which inevitably involves making mistakes – is not seen as shameful, so there is more openness to learning and no need to restrict it to only taking place in privacy. Mr. B made it clear he would prefer not to improve on something rather than accept help from someone that could lead to improvement.

Something else that stands in the way of Mr. B learning from others is the low opinion he has of others' capacity to offer him something worthwhile. He said, *'If a person was **smart enough** to say, "This is what needs to be done". . .'*. This could be seen as arrogance, but for an extremely intelligent person, it will often have been a reality that they knew more or performed better than those around them and so lost faith that others could offer them something worthwhile, making them become increasingly self-reliant.

Ending the conversation

This is how the interview ended:

ME: (p. 35) So in terms of dealing with people, the clients you deal with, the people you interview, the people you're defending, you don't feel that there would be any skills or developing of what it's like dealing with people in that sort of way that would be useful for you?

MR. B: *There may or may not be, I don't really know, but all I know is that I don't really want to be in a situation where somebody's talking to me longer than is necessary.*

ME: Well on that note I would say we could finish.

MR. B: *Thank you.*

ME: I wouldn't want to keep you longer here than is necessary.

MR. B: *Thank you, I enjoyed that, thank you very much.*

ME: Did you?

MR. B: *I did.*

ME: I'm pleased if you did.

MR. B: *It's very rare you learn something more about yourself. It's a profitable thing and I have profited from this, thank you.*

When Mr. B mentioned not wanting *'to be in a situation where somebody's talking to me longer than is necessary'*, I instantly applied that to his current conversation with me and took action to release him from the situation. When he spontaneously offered *'I enjoyed that'*, I was clearly surprised – 'Did you?'

His parting words made me realise that in spite of all Mr. B had said about hiding behind a mask, preferring to avoid conversation, and not needing people, there was still somewhere inside him an impulse to reach out, to try again, to see whether a new situation, or a new person, could bring about a conversation that might be worthwhile, 'profitable'.

The barrister's defences

Everything Mr. B did throughout his conversation with me that was contradictory, convoluted, or unkind, I see as deriving from his attempt to defend himself against pain.

He was employing the defence of 'denial' when he initially pretended that his extreme intelligence was not important to him.

He was employing the defence of 'reaction formation' when he tried to turn something painful (being labelled 'odd and difficult') into something he said he enjoys.

He was employing the defence of 'rationalisation' when he demeaned others by calling them 'idiots'. If he can portray them as having no worth, he might be able to lessen the pain of feeling he doesn't fit in with them or is rejected by them (the pain of being the 'outsider').

Mr. B's comments that criticise or undermine others are a form of attack – the 'fight' behaviour of someone who is in a state of defence rather than in a state of safety. His withdrawal and avoidance of being with others is 'flight' behaviour.

Like Shakespeare's snail, Mr. B retreats into a shell – in his case, what he calls wearing a mask. Another kind of shell is his barrister's wig and gown, which make him feel confident and esteemed.

The antidote to defences is creating a state of safety. I think my patience through this interview with Mr. B, in which I persistently showed him generosity and validation and did not myself fight, flee, or freeze, helped begin to create an experience for him of the possibility of feeling safe with me. In spite of all he said at the beginning about how he would only speak as freely as he had to me because he knew he would never see me again, he became one of only two out of all those I interviewed who took me up on my offer of a debrief and came and met with me face-to-face again for another conversation.

Do try this at home – Chapter 2 boxout

Defences we employ in conversation are ways of trying to feel safe, secure our own position, and guard against being rejected. Unfortunately, some of those defences in themselves can make the other person feel alienated and unsafe, triggering rejection. It starts to go wrong when the freedom and enjoyment of the conversation become restricted. This can escalate to the whole relationship or prospective relationship becoming restricted or jeopardised, because ultimately a person will not want to have further interactions with someone who makes them feel uncomfortable. Here are some ways you can avoid this happening.

How to avoid ruining a conversation

1 **Relinquish any pretence at being something different than what you are.** People will pick up on this and feel they can't trust you.
2 **Make an effort not to undermine (even subtly) someone you are with.** Treat whoever you are with as being worthy of respect. You can show respect by making comments that validate a person, showing you appreciate who they are and their choices and activities. If you don't appreciate them, still be respectful, but you can steer yourself away from further interaction with them.
3 **Avoid saying unkind/derogatory things about others, even if they are not present.** Saying unkind things about others makes a person realise you could also think or say such things about them, which makes them wary of you.
4 **Do not try to feel secure or increase your sense of self-worth by placing yourself 'on top' of someone else.** This includes trying to 'better' a story they tell or something they've achieved. That will not make them feel good. Also, placing yourself 'on top' can make you afraid you won't be able to keep it up and gives you further to fall.
5 **Be generous and accepting.** This encourages a person to feel more comfortable and be more honest with you.
6 **Notice if a person shows signs of feeling uncomfortable and don't repeat whatever you did when their signs of discomfort began.** Not noticing you are making others uncomfortable can make them view you as difficult to be with. This can lead to them excluding you, making you feel you are an outsider.

Notes

1 As part of the standard ethical requirements of my research, every person I interviewed first signed a consent form allowing me to audio-record, share, and publish content from our conversation provided their identity remains anonymous. This means I can mention things like a person's gender and profession but not their real name nor other personal details that could make them identifiable. I follow this rule throughout this book in any conversations I share, protecting the anonymity of the individuals involved.
2 See Falck (2020, p. 14).

3 In Falck (2021) I explain how I see Western culture as having arrived at this conflicting position in relation to intelligence and the psychology underlying it.
4 Chaudoir and Fisher (2010).
5 Dweck (2006).

References

Chaudoir, S.R. and Fisher, J.D. (2010). The Disclosure Processes Model: Understanding Disclosure Decision Making and Postdisclosure Outcomes among People Living with a Concealable Stigmatized Identity. *Psychological Bulletin*, 136(2), pp. 236–256.
Dweck, C.S. (2006). *Mindset: How You Can Fulfil Your Potential*. London: Constable & Robinson Ltd.
Falck, S. (2020). *Extreme Intelligence – Development, Predicaments, Implications*. London: Routledge.
Falck, S. (2021). *The Psychology of Intelligence*. London: Routledge.

3   Playing the game

We have seen how the barrister Mr. B employed various defences in the attempt to avoid pain or create safety for himself. Unfortunately, doing this involved making manoeuvres that were themselves likely to create more difficulty, leading to others labelling him, as he said, 'odd or difficult' and treating him as an 'outsider', which he said he hated.

Taking inspiration from *Games People Play*,[1] a book by Eric Berne, founder of Transactional Analysis, some of these manoeuvres could be formulated as 'games high-IQ adults play'. I will return to this, but first, a word about ways of playing.

Ways of playing

I see three main different ways of playing a game. One is playing for safety, to try and create safety for yourself. Another is when you are already feeling safe and are playing for enjoyment, for fun, to give and receive pleasure. The third is playing for competition, trying to win (see Figure 3.1).

This third way of playing – playing for competition – can overlap with the other two. It overlaps with the second when playing for competition is also fun and enjoyable – for example, when playing a boardgame or sport. It overlaps with the first when you might need to compete in some way to create safety for yourself, like competing against others in a job interview and trying to win so you can secure the safety of an income.

Playing for safety and playing for enjoyment do not overlap. This is because playing for enjoyment is dependent on already being in a state of safety. In other words, you can compete from a position of enjoying yourself or from a position of fighting for survival, but the position of fighting for survival rules out enjoyment – while Katniss was competing for her life in *The Hunger Games*, she was not simultaneously enjoying herself.

Confusion, misunderstanding, conflict, and distress can arise when people within the same context are playing differently from each other. For example, in a business context one person could be enjoying playing for competition, whereas another is playing for safety – for that person the stakes are higher and they feel their survival depends on being successful. In a social conversation where most participants are playing for enjoyment, someone who engages in

DOI: 10.4324/9781003029106-5

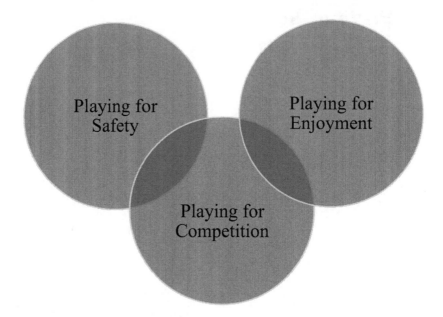

Figure 3.1 Ways of playing

the conversation as though they are in competition is likely to be experienced as offensive, and someone who engages as though they are playing for safety could be experienced as dull or baffling and inappropriate. The rest of this chapter will explore in different ways this theme of playing in conversation.

Games high-IQ adults play

Here is one such game that Mr. B, the barrister, played with me: *I can't acknowledge my high ability because that constitutes boasting, which is frowned upon, but I need recognition, so I'm going to deny I should get credit for something and that will cue you to respond with granting recognition by assuring me I should be given credit for it.* We could call this game 'stroke me'.

The 'staying on top' game is this: *My self-worth depends on maintaining a high position. I therefore feel most safe when your position is lower than mine. To reassure myself of maintaining my position, I might have to undermine your position.*

Another game in the barrister's case is this – I'll call it 'setting my own trap': *I want to confirm I am capable, but when I confirm I am capable that causes you to have high expectations of me, and I then feel pressured not to disappoint your expectation, so I am trapped into continuing to assert my capability.*

Psychoanalyst Jessica Benjamin gave another take on these sorts of patterns of interaction between people. She called them 'locked-in complementarities',[2] a term that denotes how a person can get stuck in a particular way of behaving which tends to activate in others a complementing type of behaviour. In this way it becomes a pattern (or game) in which there are only two available positions – if you're not in one of those two positions, then you're in the other.

An example of a locked-in complementarity in the barrister's case could be called judge/idiot. In this locked-in complementarity, the roles of judge and idiot are taken up by two people and continue to be occupied by the two of them, but always with the possibility that the roles they begin with could be reversed. When Mr. B said he was 'fond' of 'calling people idiots', he was placing himself in the role of judge – he was the one judging others as idiots. While he is the judge, he is not the idiot. But because he is locked-in to this way of interacting with others, there is always the risk that the other person could become the judge instead of him and then that would make him become the idiot. He expressed his fear of this to me right at the start of his conversation with me, when he said:

MR. B: *Even if you judge me it doesn't matter. You are a stranger, I'm probably never going to run into you again, so it doesn't matter.*

So although I was a stranger to Mr. B who he was meeting for the first time, he was already approaching it with the readiness to view it in these terms, and in advance he was planning his escape (he had said, 'as far as I'm concerned, this is our only meeting') so that if I did become the judge, and exposed him as the idiot, he could flee the pain of it by never having to face me again. What he said about feeling a fraud, and having imposter syndrome, and wearing a mask, were all ways of expressing this fear he had of being exposed.

Even without Mr. B telling me that this was his 'game' – perhaps without even himself realising this was his 'game' – he managed to activate a complementary role in me. When I tried to show him I was competent at my job as a psychotherapist by saying I could understand things about him that he himself couldn't understand, and when I asked him a question in a way that showed I already believed I knew what the answer was, these were behaviours on my part that showed I was accepting his role as 'judge' and trying to minimise my discomfort at being in the role of 'idiot'. So, I had become caught up in his game.

The fact Mr. B was, in his very first meeting of me, ready to see me as either judge or idiot, shows that he was not approaching me with an open mind. Instead, he was projecting onto me a game he had come prepared with. All of us do that – we project our previous 'games' onto others, assuming when we interact with someone that we will be playing the same old game again. Sigmund Freud called this 'transference',[3] and explained how we transfer onto new people we meet the memories and expectations we have developed through our previous interactions with people.

We carry around whole game strategies with us that we can employ in social interactions and even in entire relationships. The attachment patterns I explained in Chapter 1 are strategies we develop for how to manage other people, such as 'I will avoid asking you for what I need in case being needy makes you abandon me' (which is the fleeing strategy of an avoidant attachment style) or 'I will exaggerate what I need in the hope you will notice and give me some attention' (which is the fighting strategy of an anxious attachment style).

When two people get locked-in to a complementary pattern of behaviour with each other, Benjamin termed this an 'enactment'[4] – each person is repetitively acting out a role and while their positions can switch over, they always still occupy one of the two available roles. In addition to judge/idiot, some other examples of such complementarities are beauty/admirer, professor/student, master/slave, bully/victim, or one that Eric Berne named Parent/Child.

There is a power element within these complementarities, in a domination/submission type of structure. In the examples I've given of complementarities, the one named first in each pair is the dominant role, or the role with more power. I'm sure each of us can think of an example of someone who 'invites' us to play a role with them, projecting onto us their expectations that we will become their helper, their admirer, their critic, and so on. I'm sure we've all also experienced only noticing afterwards how we got almost hypnotised into accepting that role. And how we can get to a point where we don't want to be in that role anymore and we may feel the only way we can manage this is to stop interacting with that person, ending any relationship we had with them.

In the judge/idiot game, no one wants to be devalued as an idiot, so if a person picks up on the other having this attitude it might stir them to compete with the other to try to prove they are not the idiot that the other is expecting they might be. A more subtle version of this, which many high-IQ adults get locked-into, is a game of 'I am the smart one'. If two people are in a state of safety with each other, they might enjoy this game – it could be a kind of intellectual sparring that is fun and stimulating for both parties without any adverse consequences. This can be a 'playing for enjoyment' interaction that belongs in the 'Thriving' quadrant (see Chapter 1, Figure 1.1).

But it could have darker undertones when there is real power at stake. In such a game your options are to submit (*you're smart, I'm not*), or you can continue to vie to be the one who is dominant (i.e. smart). Or you might well prefer to avoid the whole hard work and unpleasantness of trying to maintain your self-worth through constantly having to compete, and choose instead to stay away from that person in future or even disengage from or avoid further social interaction in general (as reflected in the 'Hiding Self' quadrants). I have worked with clients who were traumatised by growing up with a parent who locked them into this game. In some cases the parent even used violence to try to maintain dominance over their extremely intelligent child whose abilities and questions made the parent feel threatened.

When I meet a new client, part of my job is to find out what sorts of games they might be playing – as initiator, or respondent – and to help them out of being locked into these games. Sometimes you can only understand what the game is by getting caught up in it (temporarily), as I did in my conversation with Mr. B. But once you get caught in these games, what is the way out? And can you interact with other human beings in a way that is free of these sorts of games?

Playing it straight, or 'not playing games'

In 1855 – the year before Sigmund Freud was born – Danish philosopher Søren Kierkegaard died. In his substantial life's works he had a lot to say about authenticity, describing it as a person's task in life:

> His task is: to be himself . . ., be true. That he should be true, that is, that he, himself, should be what he proclaims [to be], or at least strive to be that, or at least be honest enough to confess, about himself, that he is not that . . . [5]

In his book *The Sickness unto Death* he detailed the despair that comes from not being who you are.[6]

Being true to who you are involves getting to know who you are. Long before Kierkegaard, dated as far back as 1400 BCE in Ancient Greece, the accepted source of all wisdom was the Delphi Oracle, which had the dictum of 'Know Thyself'. Freud's life's work rested on these same principles – know yourself, and be true to yourself. He saw all neurotic problems in the patients he treated as deriving from their attempts to employ defence mechanisms – chiefly 'repression' – to hide from others and even from themselves the truth of their experiences and desires when they associated these with pain or disapproval.

Every major psychological approach since Freud has a vocabulary for expressing these same insights. For example, Carl Rogers, American founder of the humanistic Person-Centred approach, said all emotional and psychological health rested on 'congruence',[7] and 'incongruence' was the source of all problems. Psychoanalyst Donald Winnicott explained how a person gains health and vitality from living their 'true self',[8] and that developing a 'false self' to try to gain approval was what underpinned a life that felt miserable and meaningless.

The kinds of games discussed in the previous section are all forms of defence, hiding from authentic relating in an attempt to avoid discomfort or pain. I have introduced Eric Berne and Jessica Benjamin as thinkers who identified ways that people can get caught up in these sorts of problematic patterns of interpersonal relating. What did they think was the way to break out of such patterns?

For both of them, becoming aware of the way you're interacting is the first step. This usually begins by reflecting on past interactions, looking with hindsight at what was happening. Hindsight means you're no longer in the heat of the moment, so you can notice things you didn't notice at the time. Benjamin talks about stepping outside of the locked-in complementarity – that situation in which two people are enacting two roles with each other – to a third[9] position from which you transcend being involved in either of the two roles and can become curious about what was going on. When my conversation with Mr. B was over and I read the transcript of it, I was no longer involved, and with hindsight I could examine how we had interacted with each other. (The concept of 'kindsight' encourages looking back with hindsight in a way that is kind, not criticising past actions but focusing on what can be helpfully learnt from them.[10])

In the course of reflecting on something, you can develop insight into the dynamics that were in place and what your part in that was. By analysing my conversation with Mr. B, I could gain insight into the dynamics going on between us, and apply concepts like defences and games. I could develop understanding that maybe what appeared objectionable behaviour on his part really came from his attempt to keep himself safe.

An insight from Berne that can help avoid games is that instead of taking up a role in relation to other adults that follows the Parent/Child pattern (where one person is more authoritative and dominant and the other powerless), we can aim to rather take up a dynamic of Adult/Adult. This means we are striving to be equals, each with the same grown-up powers of speech and knowledge, neither one being in authority over the other, both with equal responsibility, both listening to each other and responding to each other with respect.

Building on Berne's work, American psychiatrist Thomas Anthony Harris recommended approaching all others from the position of 'I'm OK, You're OK'.[11] This means not seeing yourself as a better or worse person than anyone else. Obviously abilities, actions, choices, attitudes, and achievements differ enormously amongst people, but holding this stance depends on having compassion for people, believing everyone is doing the best they can in the conditions they are grappling with.

'I'm OK, You're OK' is the opposite of idealising others (viewing them as much better than yourself), or devaluing or demonising others (viewing them as much worse than yourself). An extremely intelligent person can have special difficulty with this because they will often have grown up either being idealised or demonised for their marked abilities and heightened sensitivities. It is hard for a person with extreme intelligence to see themselves as being neither more nor less 'OK' than others. And if their self-worth – as with Mr. B – has become dependent on their image of themselves as performing better than others, they might particularly want to hold onto seeing themselves as 'more special' than others.

Once you have been through the process of hindsight (or kindsight) and insight, the next step is to aim for foresight. This is when you go into your next interactions armed with the new insights you have gained, and can foresee what difficulties might arise. This also makes you more likely to notice in the moment of your behaviour towards someone what kind of way you are behaving. Such awareness enables you to use your insights to make informed choices about how you want to engage, what you want to say, where it's coming from in you (for example, are you playing the victim, are you playing the bully, are you playing your part in promoting Adult/Adult), and what impact it might have.

When you enter conversations aiming to be authentic, congruent, your true self, you are far less susceptible to getting caught up in problematic games, either as the initiator or the respondent. This is because overall you know who you are, you accept this, and you say what you mean. You are not being false, 'putting on a mask', being manipulative. Instead, when you interact in this kind of way with others, you can start playing for enjoyment.

Playing for enjoyment (and healing, growth, and productivity)

It might be assumed that playing, having fun, and enjoying yourself are positive things a person would strive for. But people with extreme intelligence can have a more complicated relationship with this. I have had clients who talked about how, when they were growing up, the way children had 'fun' was something they had no interest in, and they sought interaction with and validation from adults, not from their peers. Such people are very likely to still be – as Freud maintained is true of everyone – always trying to avoid pain and seek pleasure.[12] But the ways in which they do this can differ from the neurotypical majority. They might gravitate towards seeking more solitary pleasures that keep them safe from what they have experienced are activities unsuited to their abilities and sensitivities and the associated problematic interactions with others.

As mentioned above, playing for enjoyment is dependent on being in a state of safety. And an important rule of play is that there must be no adverse consequences. Play as defined in Polyvagal Theory involves 'synchronous and reciprocal behaviours between individuals',[13] where they give each other friendly social cues like face-to-face contact, smiling, making friendly vocalisations – in other words keeping the Social Engagement System activated. This signals that the behaviour involved is safe and not threatening, which prevents the nervous system from transitioning into aggression (fight) or frightened collapse (freeze). Playful behaviour acts as a neural exercise, co-regulating each other in a way that supports mental and physical health.

We strongly associate play with childhood, presuming that play is what children do and want to do. That is true, but play is not restricted to children. For example, the *Journal of Product Innovation Management* has presented strong evidence of how play practices in organisations increase psychological safety, which in turn increases play, and how together these foster higher levels of innovation.[14] Google is a fabulously successful company that designs its offices to specifically promote physical and verbal play, with ping-pong tables, climbing walls, slides, sports facilities, and areas with comfortable café facilities and whiteboards for collaborative discussion and brainstorming.

Between consenting adults, a wonderful form of play is mutual sexual expression and exploration, both physically and verbally. Enjoyment of sex increases with increased playfulness between the partners, activating doses of oxytocin that promote well-being.[15]

Play is also therapeutic, promoting healing and growth. Neuropsychoanalyst and prolific author Allan Schore emphasises 'safe surprises' as the essence of what is therapeutic:

> [P]lay amplifies joy, excitement, and . . . surprise. A positive state in turn allows individuals to experience a situation as safe, to feel unrestrained, to take risks, to explore novel pathways, and to be creative. . . . [T]he positive

arousal of surprise is central to all forms of exploration and play and is associated with increasing safety and trust. Psychoanalyst Philip Bromberg has written extensively about the critical role of 'safe surprises' in therapy . . . that allows the self to grow.[16]

Given all the benefits of play, I strongly believe in the importance of recovering, and cultivating, the art of play in adulthood. This can introduce into personal and professional interpersonal interaction an otherwise absent enjoyment, creativity, connectivity, and productivity.

Playing for safety, which includes 'playing it safe'

It is important to realise that artifice, dishonesty, and manipulative games can be the best strategy a person has been able to find for trying to keep safe. Lying is a way of protecting yourself against the reaction you fear you might get if you were to tell the truth. The false self develops to protect the true self. Such behaviours are all forms of defence.

Reacting to someone's defences can get you caught in a relational merry-go-round, never getting anywhere. It's better, therefore, to avoid engaging with whatever form the defence takes. Instead, communicate with what you perceive as the other person's inner true self, believing it is there, however hidden. Thinking of Shakespeare's snail, you do not try to have a conversation with the shell or involve yourself with commenting on the features of the shell – how tough it is or how pretty it is or how all you can see is the shell. Rather, you speak gently and soothingly and acceptingly to what is hiding inside the shell, believing that if you create safe conditions, that part will begin to feel comfortable enough to emerge again with its tender horns out like antennae scanning for safety.

If you beat against the shell in frustration or anger, that tender inner part will definitely not emerge; it will retract even more firmly 'with pain', and for even longer fear to 'creep forth again'.

A person with extreme intelligence often experiences that their talents and achievements create a dazzling shell that distracts others. Such a person can 'play it safe' by staying inside the shell and letting everyone else amuse themselves with the features of the shell. But such a person can become increasingly distressed and angry, because the shell is the 'false self', and the more this attracts praise from others, the more they hate the praise and the more lost and isolated and desperate they can feel inside.

If such a person begins to hate their achievements and even wants to give up on their talents, they often meet with shocked disbelief. And if they have some form of breakdown or develop destructive addictions or behave badly (all of which are attempts to find regulation), people tend to say they cannot understand how someone so successful (someone with such a stunning shell) could crash.

Playing along

A version of playing for safety is 'playing along'. Here is an example. In several Middle Eastern and Asian cultures there is a fear of a supernatural malevolent force called 'the evil eye', which is based in jealousy. This means you must be careful not to show off things that are good because the envious evil eye is watching and could attack your good things, causing you misfortune. When Hindu babies are born, to prevent people from praising the beauty of the baby and thereby attracting the attention of the evil eye, a black spot called a *kala tikka* is drawn on the baby's face to mar its beauty. This is a kind of game, because everybody involved knows the black spot is not real, that underneath it the baby is this very perfectly beautiful creature. But everyone plays along with the game. It performs a function that could be necessary in that society, which is to make people feel safer, that they have protected themselves against the evil eye.

We do not need to believe in any concept of a supernatural force to recognise the existence of envy-related dangers: ordinary human beings easily experience unpleasant envious feelings when they see good things another person has and might try to spoil it for that person.[17] There are well-established terms for this in other cultures also, such as 'cutting tall poppies' in Australia and *Schadenfreude* in Europe.[18] Protecting against envious attacks of this kind might well be the root of the prohibition against boasting, when high-achieving children are dissuaded from drawing attention to the good they have done.

By providing an outward sign that the good thing is not all that good and therefore does not need to be envied, the *kala tikka* makes a bid for protection. In this sense the *kala tikka* is a wise ritual – it makes those who might be envious feel better at seeing the ugly paint marring the beautiful new baby. It has already been spoiled, so they won't feel the need to do any further spoiling. With that need removed, the parents feel their baby is safer. Everyone plays along with the game, and it makes things go more smoothly within that society.

In any existing system – families, societies, organisations, whole countries – there is an already-established culture. Individuals with extreme intelligence are very quick to detect features and patterns in systems that relate concretely to efficiency of functioning, productivity, and progress. Often they are eager to point out what they've noticed and to suggest improvements, even when they experience these are not welcomed.

In such situations, what the extremely intelligent person has not understood is that inefficient-seeming processes – like the *kala tikka* – are there for a reason. Even if they are imperfect, they provide those inside the system with a sense of safety, a familiar routine, and a security that they know how things work. If these are attacked, the system retaliates.

If you want to secure your employment, begin by playing along with how things are and follow the procedures. Once you have developed a strong basis of safety within that system – for example, you have passed your probation period and your employment contract has been made permanent – then you could find wise ways to begin making suggestions for how the system could be improved.

It can be hard to see the difference between playing along with something and being inauthentic. An extremely intelligent person often has a blunt honesty, a tendency to blurt out what they notice. They can feel they are being inauthentic if they do not say what they see is wrong, or they feel that they are being false or unprincipled if they go along with something they can see is flawed. But if you don't at least play along with it for long enough to build relationships and have others begin to trust you, no one will listen to you when you make your clever suggestions; they will experience you as a threat and dismiss what you say or dismiss you from the job.

Playing along, then, means that you can see that a conversation (like small talk, which I discuss in Chapter 6), an activity, a procedure, or a whole system is not profound or efficient – or even, you might think, useful – and yet you can respect that it is *necessary*, and so you go along with it, at least for as long as doing so supports a bigger goal.

The rules of the game – authenticity revisited

During one of her sessions with me, a client of mine was crying over the fact that she didn't know whether she would ever be able to really be herself and have someone else accept that and love that. She said, 'Am I just too direct and blunt and will that eventually always end things with people? Or do I have to be fake, so that I'm not being blunt and direct?'

'What do you mean by fake?' I asked her. 'If you're giving the same authentic message to people about who you really are, but just delivering it in a way that is less blunt and more tactful, then you're not being fake.'

I gave her the analogy of driving a car. You can drive your car authentically to the destination you want to get to, but you cannot drive it in a straight line: you have to follow the roads that have been made, and you have to obey the traffic rules, stop at the red lights, slow down at amber, and yield at times to other drivers. You have to expect that you won't be able to see what's ahead of you at a blind corner, that you will sometimes get stuck behind other vehicles, that you have to be careful at a hairpin bend. And when conditions change, like it is raining, icy, or there is low visibility, you have to adapt to keep safe, changing the way you drive in accordance with the conditions. I said to my client, 'Adapting in these ways, when driving, isn't so terrible, is it? When it comes to interpersonal relating, why not also accept there will be rules to observe, and adapt to that?'

She said, 'But that takes so much hard work. I just want to be able to be myself.'

I said,

> Why do you expect when you're interacting with others that you should just be able to do whatever you want? Relationships, like driving, do

require ongoing alertness. Once you've learned the rules of the road and got your driver's licence, you can get where you want to go in a way that feels natural and is effective, but you accept that you need to stay alert, at all times, because if you don't, even once you've got your licence, you can still crash. Why not accept that with relationships also?

Playing the long game

High-IQ people are often in a hurry. They think fast, talk fast, learn fast. They want to understand everything, master things, move on to the next. I have met several who have dabbled in each of a few different degrees but never finished any of them because they reached a point where they felt they already knew enough. But this style can favour the gaining of superficial knowledge. Also, it means such a person does not gain the qualification that the systems of the world – however flawed or inferior they may be – require as entrance criteria to occupations that in themselves could provide all kinds of worthwhile longer-term benefits.

Improving at relationships involves gaining experiential knowledge. This means going through experiences in real time. You can't fast-forward. You can't get the summary and move on – there's no Blinkist for getting to know a person. If you want to improve at interpersonal communication, you need to practice. It takes time.

But what's the rush? You can learn, develop, grow, and mature. You don't have to know everything right now. Reputations take a long time to build. Friendships and relationships that are rich and solid take a long time to build. If you want the best and deepest rewards, you have to be in it for the long haul, play the long game. So, it is worth persevering, and losing the impatience. You don't have to do everything correctly already. Tomorrow is another day.

The whole of life as a game

Tomorrow is always another day, until it is not. For every one of us a point will come when our life – or at least, depending on your views, our mortal incarnation – will end. And because of this, in a sense we're all playing a game of immortality when we generally go about our daily life believing in the continuity of things as though we have an open-ended future ahead of us. We get so absorbed in this game that we manage to be surprised, shocked even, whenever we receive news of a death, as though this is a terrible misfortune rather than an inevitability.

This is something like the ancient concept of 'maya', found in Buddhism and Hinduism. Maya is often interpreted as meaning that the world is an illusion, although the more correct meaning may be that the world is an appearance.[19] It refers to the fact that we cover over the more profound, less visible, and more spiritual mysteries and realities of life and death with things that are more visible, that appear to us and take up our attention, and we fully involve ourselves with many worldly pursuits and concerns and care about material possessions as though all those things matter, not seeing the truth that all of it will pass away.

Even though it will all pass away, and we can cultivate a deeper connection with and reverence for what is greater than our daily worldly concerns, we can still choose to accept and play along with being interested in our worldly existence. We can allow ourselves to be absorbed in and enjoy that while we have it.

Something of an antidote to worrying about this is the Zen philosophy of being in the moment, and letting that moment be what it is, giving it your attention – this is my rice bowl I have eaten from, and now I am washing the bowl. I can feel the satisfaction of the meal that is currently filling and nourishing me, feel the warm water run over my hands, watch the surface of the bowl becoming clean, and be grateful for these things. For this moment, that is enough.

Do try this at home – Chapter 3 boxout

Play is engaging in an activity only for the purpose of enjoyment, with no adverse consequences. The essence of play is safe surprises: saying or doing something the other person doesn't expect, but which is harmless and tends to provoke laughter.

Here is an example, involving something silly I do with my husband. I go up to him with two mints in my mouth, kiss him, and during the kiss, surprise him by transferring a mint into his mouth, so we are left with having one each. That is the pattern.

One day while he is sitting at his desk I go up to him and do that. As my tongue pushes the mint into his mouth, I feel him receiving the mint into his mouth but then pushing it back towards mine. I resist, pushing it back to him, and he resists, so that the mint is caught between our mouths, and I have started laughing because it is so surprising to have him resist it like this and push it back to me.

My laughter makes me pull away from him, and I say, 'Don't you want it?' Looking me straight in the eye, with a huge smile, he says, 'Yes I do!' That makes me laugh even more, because it makes no sense that he does want it yet has resisted receiving it. So, it's nonsense, which is fun.

I kiss him again, and by now we are both laughing so much that it becomes something of a feat to manage the transfer and we almost drop both mints. But we succeed, then pull apart, looking at each other, a mint in each of our mouths, both laughing.

The laughter – and kiss – creates a burst of feel-good hormones. His behaviour disrupted a usual pattern between us, introducing novelty that is rejuvenating. This induces in me positive feelings towards him and more interest in him because I like experiencing that he comes up with things I don't expect and which are fun – safe surprises.

Playing like this shows both of us that we accept each other and don't even have to make sense. This strengthens our bond, reinforcing the freedom and trust between us. And it builds a new memory together that makes each of us smile.

How to play

Extracting the elements from this example to identify the principles of play, here are some instructions on how to play:

1   **Think of a pattern in behaviour between you and someone else.** This would be a sequence – verbal or physical, or both – that occurs regularly between you.
2   **Think of a way to disrupt it.** Identify something you could say or do that the other person wouldn't expect, but which is harmless, which would disrupt your regular pattern.
3   **Perform the disruption.** Ensure you do this when the other person is relaxed, not busy or stressed or in a hurry to go somewhere.
4   **Allow the laughter to erupt.** Welcome the feel-good hormones, make eye contact, and mutually enjoy the moment.
5   **Give no explanation for having behaved this way.** Let it make no sense.
6   **Acknowledge what was good about this.** Later, even days later, when the other person is not expecting it, show them you're remembering it – mention it and let them know you thought it was fun. Even just send them a text out of the blue that says, 'Right now I'm thinking about . . . [describe it] . . . and it's making me smile!'

Notes

1 Berne (1964).
2 Benjamin (2009).
3 Freud (1917).
4 Benjamin (2009).
5 Kierkegaard (1850, pp. 234–235). First published in 1848. This edition is published in 1992 by Princeton University Press.
6 Kierkegaard (1849). Published first in Danish in 1849. Translation published in 1989.
7 Rogers (1959, 1961).
8 Winnicott (1960).
9 Benjamin (2009).
10 NotSalmon (2011).
11 Harris (1973).
12 Freud (1920).
13 Porges (2017, p. 22).
14 Mukerjee and Metiu (2022).
15 Carter (1992).

16 Schore (2017, p. 131).
17 I write more about this in Falck (2020, pp. 90–92), and Falck (2021, pp. 54–55).
18 For more about this, see Falck (2020, pp. 90–92).
19 See Mitra (2020).

References

Benjamin, J. (2009). A Relational Psychoanalysis Perspective on the Necessity of Acknowledging Failure in Order to Restore the Facilitating and Containing Features of the Intersubjective Relationship (The Shared Third). *The International Journal of Psychoanalysis*, 90(3), pp. 441–450.

Berne, E. (1964). *Games People Play*. New York: Ballantine Books.

Carter, C.S. (1992). Oxytocin and Sexual Behavior. *Neuroscience & Biobehavioral Reviews*, 16(2), pp. 131–144. doi:10.1016/s0149-7634(05)80176-9.

Falck, S. (2020). *Extreme Intelligence – Development, Predicaments, Implications*. London: Routledge.

Falck, S. (2021). *The Psychology of Intelligence*. London: Routledge.

Freud, S. (1917). Transference. In J. Strachey (ed.) *The Standard Edition of the Complete Psychological Works of Sigmund Freud Volume 1* (Reprint 1991). London: Penguin Books, pp. 482–500.

Freud, S. (1920). Beyond the Pleasure Principle. In J. Strachey (ed.) *The Standard Edition of the Complete Psychological Works of Sigmund Freud Volume XVIII* (Reprint 2001). London: Vintage.

Harris, T.A. (1973). *I'm OK, You're OK*. London: Random House.

Kierkegaard, S. (1849). *The Sickness unto Death*. Translated with an Introduction and Notes by Alastair Hannay. London: Penguin.

Kierkegaard, Søren. (1850). *Kierkegaard's Writings, XX, Volume 20: Practice in Christianity* (Revised edition). Edited and translated by Howard V. Hong and Edna H. Hong. Princeton: Princeton University Press.

Mitra, A. (2020). Maya: A Conceptual History. *Prabuddha Bharata*, Special Issue (January): Visions of Advaita, 125(1), pp. 266–275.

Mukerjee, J. and Metiu, A. (2022). Play and Psychological Safety: An Ethnography of Innovative Work. *Journal of Product Innovation Management*, 39(3), pp. 394–418. doi:10.1111/jpim.12598.

NotSalmon. (2011). *A Life Quote about Viewing Your Past with Kindsight-Karen Salmansohn* [online]. Available at: www.notsalmon.com/2011/05/26/view-your-life-with-kindsight/ [Accessed 16 July 2022].

Porges, S.W. (2017). *The Pocket Guide to the Polyvagal Theory: The Transformative Power of Feeling Safe*. New York: W.W. Norton & Company.

Rogers, C. (1959). A Theory of Therapy, Personality and Interpersonal Relationships as Developed in the Client-Centered Framework. In S. Koch (ed.) *Psychology: A Study of a Science. Vol. 3: Formulations of the Person and the Social Context*. New York: McGraw Hill.

Rogers, C. (1961). *On Becoming a Person: A Therapist's View of Psychotherapy*. London: Constable.

Schore, A.N. (2017). Playing on the Right Side of the Brain. *American Journal of Play*, 9(2), pp. 105–142.

Winnicott, D.W. (1960). Ego Distortion in Terms of True and False Self. In *The Maturational Processes and the Facilitating Environment* (Reprint 1990). London: Karnac, pp. 140–152.

Part II
Skills

Seven essential communication skills

4 Explaining the seven essential communication skills

Every communication, with anyone, regardless of context, goes through a cycle. Even for Hillary Clinton. During an ABC News interview in 2003, she spoke of her marriage with Bill Clinton and the connection between them that had made it possible for them to overcome many troubles, including his infamous dalliance with a young White House intern during his US presidency. Hillary said that she and Bill 'started a conversation in the spring of 1971, and more than 30 years later we're still talking'.[1] That makes it sound like a conversation that has been continuous through several decades. And in long relationships, in a sense that can be true. But still, it's like a Netflix series – however long the series might last, each episode has a beginning, a middle, and an end. Similarly, every episode of communication – whether a one-off or part of a long series – goes through a cycle from beginning to end, whether this takes place through one brief exchange of text messages or during an hours-long chat over a good bottle of wine. Figure 4.1 depicts this cycle of communication.

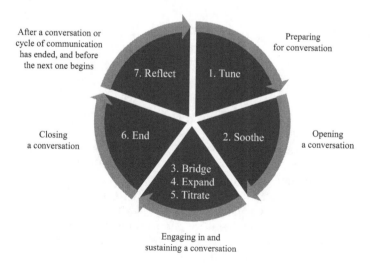

Figure 4.1 The IT'S BETTER cycle of communication

DOI: 10.4324/9781003029106-7

If the communication is brief, the cycle involved might be partial or trun-cated. My conceptualisation of the most full and complete of communication cycles is that it goes through five phases (Preparing, Opening, Engaging & Sustaining, Closing, Reflecting). And grouped within these five phases, I have identified seven essential communication skills that can help improve cycles of communication, no matter what the context.

The seven skills are grouped as follows: one skill for the Preparing phase (Tune), one skill for the Opening phase (Soothe), three skills for the Engag-ing & Sustaining phase (Bridge, Expand, Titrate), one skill for the Closing phase (End), and one skill for what happens after the ending of that cycle and before the opening of the next cycle (Reflect).

We can build from the seven skills an acronym of 'it's better', as follows:

I – 'I' is what you always begin with. This means that you are taking active responsibility for your part in the communication – as in, 'I am the one who will Tune, and Soothe, and Bridge, etc . . .'
T – Tune
S – Soothe
B – Bridge
E – Expand
TT – Titrate
E – End
R – Reflect

A way to remember this, then, is to think that if you use these essential skills for communication, it's better. The rest of the chapter is divided into seven sections, one section for explaining each skill.

Preparing phase

Skill no. 1: Tune

Before an orchestra plays, every time, it prepares. Each member of the orchestra must first tune their instrument. Without this, when the performance begins the instruments will produce sounds that jar with each other rather than make beautiful music together. It is the same with any episode of communication. Tuning is the nonverbal preparation you engage in before the spoken part of a conversation begins. For the best chance of communicating effectively, first prepare by tuning in to the other person.

In an orchestra, tuning begins with one instrument – traditionally an oboe, perhaps then taken up by a violin, or piano – playing the note A. This sets the standard for the pitch or number of vibrations per second that the other instru-ments will need to match if they want to play in harmony with each other. Depending on your place in the orchestra, either you would be the one setting the pitch for the others to follow or you would need to adjust your instrument to match another instrument.

In episodes of communication, who sets the pitch is determined by factors like hierarchy between speakers, style of relating, and context. In the context of an orchestra the instruments tune to A, but in the context of bands they tune to B flat. Becoming aware of what influences the way the pitch of communication gets set will help you get a sense of how you and others are affecting each other. There is a great story about how the CFO of Lucasfilm found Steve Jobs 'arrogant and prickly',[2] so for a forthcoming meeting with Jobs and the other stakeholders for a big deal they were negotiating, the CFO told his colleagues he would arrive a little later than the advertised start time for the meeting so he could walk in and show Jobs that he was the one with the authority. What happened was that when he arrived, he found Steve Jobs had started the meeting on time, without him, and had already taken full control of the meeting. In this way the CFO's plan for how to ensure he would be the one who set the pitch backfired, because Jobs had such an innate presumption of authority that he easily dominated.

Tuning to another musical instrument involves two things: listening to the sound of that instrument, and adjusting your own instrument to match it. In communication, you cannot change how another person behaves and communicates. You might be able to influence it, but you cannot control it. What you do have control over, is adjusting your own behaviour and communication to bring it more in tune with that of the other person.

Tuning to another person involves noticing their body language, and the pace, pitch, and tone of their voice, and the kind of vocabulary they are using, and adjusting your own to better match theirs. Often this happens quite automatically. When I was a child and would see an expression on my father's face that involved one eyebrow raised above the other in a scowl, I knew instantly that he was in a bad mood and I would adjust my behaviour to be cautious and keep a low profile. Last week I had a one-to-one Zoom call hosted by a colleague in Holland. As soon as her face came onto my screen I saw her big smile, her whole posture directed towards being attentive to me, and heard her say, 'Well hello there!' in a robust yet lilting voice that was full of fun and mischief. It was the warmest of welcomes, a clear invitation to play. It gave me an instant burst of joy and produced a matching huge smile in me. I felt her openness and resilience, knew we would be able to speak very freely with each other, and I felt both relaxed and energised, with enthusiasm for the adventure of conversation that lay ahead. This reminds me of the practice of improvisation in jazz bands, where the players make up the music as they go along by very carefully listening and responding to each other's playing.

After tuning, a musician gets into a physical posture that's comfortable, gets their mind focused on what sort of piece is coming, takes a breath, then starts playing. This is relevant for conversation also. Consider not just your physical position but also the position from which you will be communicating: which role is forefront – for example, you as friend, or parent, or colleague, or leader? Get your mind focused on what sort of conversational piece lies ahead. Is it exploratory, goal-directed, on a certain topic or not, within set limits or not? Take a breath – follow the 'How to breathe' guidelines in the boxout at the end of Chapter 1. Also follow the 'How to listen' guidelines in the boxout at the end of this chapter. Now you are ready to play.

Opening phase

Skill no. 2: Soothe

Conversation can be like finding treasure, or it can be like being led into danger. In many myths and fairytales and other stories there is a goal of finding the treasure, but first a danger must be averted. It is the same in conversation.

Let's imagine a typical storybook scenario: a dangerous beast is positioned at the gateway to the treasure. In conversation, the dangerous beast is the autonomic nervous system – remember that in interpersonal interactions the autonomic nervous system is always present, ready to jump to a state of defence, and we want to avoid this, by creating a state of safety instead. How do you gain safe passage through the gateway so that you can access the treasure?

You soothe the beast.

Soothing the beast is achieved in different ways in different stories. You might have to stroke it to relax and befriend it. You might have to give it its favourite thing to eat which satisfies it and distracts it from causing you trouble, or give it a magical potion which sends it blissfully to sleep, clearing your way to the treasure. In Figure 4.2, Orpheus, a character from Greek mythology, plays his lyre with such magical sweetness that he subdues the innate hostilities – or defences – of all the different animals, birds, and reptiles who gather around him. In other words, he soothes them. (See if you can spot the snail in the picture, looking comfortable outside its shell, which we can see as representing Shakespeare's snail.)

When you begin a conversation, view the other person as harbouring treasure which you have to find by soothing the beast. How do you soothe?

In many cultures, conversations begin with offering a gift. In Egypt and Turkey mint tea is offered, like a magical potion that soothes the beast. In almost any country, when you go into someone's home, you bring a little gift – like a bottle of wine if you're going to a dinner party. Even when you're not offering a physical gift, you can begin a conversation by offering a gift in the form of something pleasing that you say. This could involve offering a compliment to the other person (but only give an authentic compliment, something you genuinely feel), or simply saying something positive about being pleased to see them. Be aware of how you're using your voice – remember from Chapter 1 that prosody is a soothing way of speaking, and use a tone that is gentle and receptive to the other person rather than abrasive or domineering.

When you have soothed the beast and gained passage through the gateway, there is further to go before you reach the treasure, and this will be detailed with the next skills. But remember that once soothed, the beast does not stay soothed forever.

Throughout a conversation, remain aware of the presence of the beast. Be alert to when it may be awakening and soothe again so that you can continue

Figure 4.2 Soothe[3]

to avert the danger and gain access to the treasure. Some simple tools for soothing include these:

- *Show courtesy*. Approach a person with respect for whatever state they might be in. ('Is this a good time for . . . ?' 'Would you mind if I join in?') Give people choices. ('When would it suit you to . . . ?' 'How would you be most comfortable approaching that?') Notice what someone has said and acknowledge it. Say 'excuse me', 'please', and 'thank you'. Be quick to say 'sorry' if something has not gone well.

- *Make the other person feel more comfortable.* Two wonderful friends of mine had a car breakdown in France and realised the nearest place they could go for help was within a nudist colony. So they removed all their clothes to ensure whoever they approached for help would feel comfortable with them.

- *Show appreciation.* When you genuinely like something about a person or what they've said, tell them. Be specific. ('I like the way you spoke up in that meeting; it was brave of you. I would like to be more courageous in meetings.')

- *Look for the positive angle.* You might well notice a negative signal from someone or negative interpretation of what they're saying (as I did during my conversation with Mr. B), but don't point that out and dwell on it – let it go. Approach others from a stance of 'I'm OK, You're OK'. Choose to look for the best in a person and speak to the positive, thinking of any negative signs as emanating from the beast who needs to be calmed.

- *In advance of meeting someone or going to a social gathering, collect for yourself a few soothing topics of conversation that you can be ready to draw on when needed.* These are safe topics that you will find it easy to talk about, such as things about yourself you're happy to disclose or interests of yours – as long as they are designed to give the other person an easy way to join in with the conversation. In other words, topics you're comfortable talking about, which you think the other person is likely to be able to relate to and also feel comfortable about. Some typical (and lazy) safe topics that people use as soothers (and can get bored by) are commenting on the weather, asking about or offering holiday plans, and commenting on public events or sports that are covered in the media and which other people are likely to be aware of or have an opinion on. You might enjoy thinking of ways of being more creative than that. Think of any non-contentious topic which offers different possible angles of exploration, and begin by showing where you are with it. For example, 'You know, I'm thinking of hiring a boat to go down the Amazon river. What do you think of that idea? I'd love to hear anything you know about planning a trip like that, from your experiences or anyone else you know of who's done anything similar?' Being open-minded, being playful, and showing the other person you're interested in having their input are good ways to soothe.

Developing tools for soothing makes conversation go better, because when you are generous and make someone else feel comfortable, they will usually reciprocate by doing the same for you. (And you most likely won't even have to take off all your clothes.)

Engaging & Sustaining phase

Skill no. 3: Bridge

When you talk to another person, by virtue of being another person they are in a physical position different from your own. Your physical positions could be geographically far apart, such as a phonecall or Zoom conversation between individuals across the world from each other. But even when lying in the arms of the person you're talking to, although you are in much greater proximity, you are still in different physical positions: they're in their body, and you're in yours.

For each person, being inside their own body is just the start of the different position involved. Each person is also inside their own mind. How, then, do you reach from where you are, to where the other person is?

You build a bridge.

What is in a person's mind can never be fully accessed by another person – people cannot read each other's minds. In Star Trek the Vulcan race has this fantasy power, which they call 'mind melding'. For the rest of us, we need to search for clues about what is in a person's mind from what they say and how they behave. It's a bit like Figure 4.3.

Figure 4.3 Bridge

The person in the image is some distance away, in fog, so it's hard for you to see them. And from where they are, you will be as hard for them to see. To see each other better, one or both of you must walk towards the other. In conversation you do this with words, building a bridge that allows you and the other person to draw nearer and become clearer to each other.

Here are three bridge-building methods, which I will elaborate on:

1   Say something (soothing) that relates to what you imagine the other person's situation is like for them.
2   Give away information about yourself (for free).
3   Ask an open question.

Let's imagine you're at a social gathering, which is a situation many very high-IQ individuals dread. But there you are, standing on your own, feeling awkward. You see someone who is a stranger to you – as unknown as the figure in the image. You can begin building a bridge by showing an interest in what things are like for that person at the position they are in. Avoid assumptions, such as saying something like, 'You must be feeling . . . [bored, excited, terrified, thrilled]'. Because you don't know what their experience is. You can guess, but you don't know which of the many options is accurate. And if you get it wrong, you will not have made one further step towards them on a bridge, you will have made them recede one step further away from you into the fog.

Instead, observe the available cues, and say something relevant to what you're noticing. But with the proviso that you should choose to say something that aims to soothe their inner beast rather than make it jump to defence. So, for example, if the person looks nervous, instead of saying, 'It looks like you're a bit lost' (which highlights their discomfort), say, 'I wonder whether you're feeling as lost as I am?' (which helps them feel more comfortable because they are discovering that someone else is feeling something similar).

In this example, you've also given away information about yourself – you've revealed that you're feeling lost. Remember that from their position, *you* are the one standing in the fog, hidden, what is in your mind unknown and unknowable to them unless you offer them a glimpse into it. When you are with another person, follow the principle of being generous: give away information about yourself for free. Rather than waiting to be asked about yourself, spontaneously initiate offering information about yourself.

Offer information not only on content (facts about yourself) but also process (how you're experiencing or thinking about something right now). So you could say,

> The last social gathering I was at was a family birthday [fact]. Everyone ended up arguing, so I'm happy that at least if tonight is boring, it won't

be as bad as that was! [shows how you're feeling] But just in case it does go wrong, I've been planning my exit strategy [shows what you're thinking].

This gives the other person several possible angles they could respond to. The more you show about yourself, the more steps you are taking towards them on the bridge, making yourself more visible to the other person, and the more comfortable you make them to take steps towards you, showing more of themselves to you.

In addition to showing more about yourself, you can build a bridge by asking more about the other person. Asking an open question means saying something that invites description, elaboration, exploration, which gives the best chance of inviting the other person to take a few steps on the bridge towards you, making themselves clearer to you. Closed questions lead only to yes/no answers (e.g. 'Do you . . . ?', 'Is it . . . ?', 'Are you . . . ?'). The other person might answer yes or no and then spontaneously elaborate further. But a person who is not chatty could just say yes or no and then go silent, which puts you back where you started, with them a distance away from you, in the fog.

Open questions begin with 'how', 'what', 'tell me . . .'. Here is an example: 'How does this social gathering/event compare with the last one you were at?' This open question also provides a specific focus that the person can respond to, and one which is something they will be able to relate to. If you say something like, 'What do you think the chemical composition is of that drink they're serving?', that would also provide a specific focus, but one which the other person is unlikely to know what to say about, unless they happen to be a mixologist. By referring to other social gatherings/events they've been to, you are referring to something you are sure they will be familiar with, which puts them on safe ground. This encourages them to respond, taking a step on the bridge towards you, emerging from the fog as they begin to give you information about who they are, how they see things, where they're coming from, which you can further build on in the conversation.

While you are building a bridge by saying things about the other person's situation, giving away information about yourself (for free), and asking open questions, it helps further if you also simultaneously employ the next two important skills – Expand, and Titrate.

Skill no. 4: Expand

'Expand' means 'become or make larger or more extensive'.[4] Whenever you're talking to anyone, it helps to expand your awareness beyond the immediate conversation you are having with that individual at that point in time. Every person is part of a system and exists within a historical context. You are never just talking to one individual. They are connected with all the people in their lives, their families and friends and workplace colleagues, the culture they have been brought up in and any additional culture they have been most exposed to, the education they have had, and the history that brought them to where they are right now.

In terms of cultural context, every culture has some basic forms of etiquette that make social interactions go more smoothly within that culture if they are adhered to, or cause awkwardness or offence if they are contravened. (For example, in England or the US burping in company is considered rude, whereas in China and Taiwan burping after a meal is considered a form of flattery to your host, demonstrating your enjoyment of the food.) For this reason, it is worth familiarising yourself with the basic etiquette of the culture with which you are interacting. There are many resources you can seek out on this, which will give guidance on when and how it is appropriate in different cultures to do things like begin a friendship or discuss money or show sexual interest in someone. Cultural practices are always evolving, so being alert to this can help you navigate social situations without blundering into expressing or acting on outdated assumptions. See the endnote for an online resource that accesses a constantly evolving international database that can provide a starting point for developing this kind of awareness.[5] Another resource is *Cultural Intelligence: Surviving and Thriving in the Global Village.*[6]

Apart from general culture, there are many other factors that will affect what a person's concerns are, what their vulnerabilities are, and how they will hear what you say. For example, are they an only child? Or an eldest sibling who is used to taking responsibility, or a youngest sibling who is used to following the lead of others? Are they used to being treated as though they are fantastic, or as though they are inadequate? Are they part of an ethnic minority? Being black, being Jewish, being an immigrant, or coming from a family where any of these applied will affect how a person expects to be treated, how they view you, and how the beast could be awakened within them and endanger your conversation.

A way to soothe this beast is to keep employing the skills already described of tuning, soothing, and bridging, to help a person feel noticed and accepted, help them feel their situation is being taken into account, or at least avoid saying things that show total ignorance of or insensitivity to their situation. Anthony O'Hare, a character in a Jojo Moyes novel,[7] manages to say something that is very offensive to another character, Jennifer Stirling. He is a journalist traumatised from working in a war zone in the Congo. At the end of a dinner party in Jennifer's comfortable and wealthy French Riviera home, Anthony – not realising she is within earshot – calls her a 'spoiled little *tai-tai*' who has 'not an original thought in her head'.[8]

Getting things wrong is what creates dramatic tension in novels and film, where characters are deliberately put together who get these things wrong. This is also the basis of a lot of comedy. Clowns are humorous figures whose conduct relies on one central premise: 'clowns don't get it.'[9] However much you try to educate and prepare yourself, you can never know in advance what another person's every sensitivity could be. And sometimes they themselves won't know: we have all had the experience of reacting to something in a way we didn't expect and don't quite understand or don't understand in that moment. It can take some time to identify how and why something triggered us, something which called our inner beast to action.

When you are at a distance, like watching a comic performance, you can vicariously enjoy someone else's blunder: it creates a nervous tension and awkwardness that provokes a release through laughter. But when it is not a performance you are viewing from a safe distance, when it happens in real life, it's not so funny. Especially when you are the person who has blundered – what then?

Even if something disastrous is said or inadvertently stumbled into, all is not lost. What has happened is a rupture in the bridge you've been working to build, and when there is a rupture we don't have to give up, fall irretrievable into the chasm – we can perform a repair.[10] See 'How to repair' in the Chapter 7 boxout. But here, in summary, I will say you can repair by using all the same skills already introduced: run through them again – Tune, Soothe, Bridge.

Tune in to what's happening for the other person – for example, if they appear offended, adjust yourself to this, don't ignore it, and don't try to race on with the conversation in the hope it will go away. Instead, slow down and acknowledge there has been a rupture ('Oh dear, I think I've said the wrong thing'). Then Soothe – say something intended to calm. A simple 'I'm sorry' shows courtesy by being ready to apologise for your part in the rupture. And do more bridging – offer some information about yourself for free ('I've never been in that situation before'), and ask an open question ('I'd really like it if you could tell me more about how that is for you?').

In the example I gave from the Jojo Moyes novel, that blunder begins a lifelong love affair between the two characters involved, Anthony and Jennifer. Characters offending each other but then going on to fall in love is a not uncommon trope in stories.

Skill no. 5: Titrate

The skills introduced so far get you started on a conversation with a person. But there is more to it than simply whether you do something or not. There is also a question of how much you do of something. Like giving away information about yourself for free, as part of the Bridge skill. How do you know what is enough to say in any given situation, or how much is too much?

You titrate.

'Titrate' is a term from chemistry. Titration is when you add droplets of a known substance to another substance, observing that substance's reaction and determining its composition by how it reacts (see Figure 4.4). This is a good analogy for effective communication.

Imagine that the pipette in the image is you, and the beaker is another person, and the liquids are contents of speech. You can offer a droplet of speech in a measured quantity and observe what the reaction is. If the reaction is favourable, you can offer another droplet. You can keep doing this – offering droplets, and observing the reaction.

Figure 4.4 Titrate

A favourable reaction is when a person looks comfortable and interested. Signs of this are giving you eye contact, smiling, having a relaxed posture, stepping or leaning towards you, their physical gestures/body position mirroring your own, and they offer more conversational content themselves. By contrast, an unfavourable reaction is when a person does not offer further conversational content, goes quiet, shuts down, becomes tense, uncomfortable, nervous, tapping a foot or fidgeting, their eyes glaze over, they do not hold eye contact, they start looking away from you in other directions. This means you are no longer holding their attention, and they are probably looking for distractions or an escape route. They might step or lean away from you.

We can take the titration analogy further. We can say that you have control over the composition of the droplets you offer, because you can choose what you do or do not say. We can also say that you never have control over the other person's reaction, because their full psychological composition is unknown. If you know your conversational partner well, you get good at predicting their reactions. But they could still surprise you. You could of course also surprise yourself by what you find yourself saying. And in great conversation, you would hope to enable 'safe surprises',[11] because that is what makes conversation fun, stimulating, adventurous, and educational. The more unknown your conversational partner is to you, the more carefully you would want to measure the droplets you offer and test out the reaction.

Here is an example of applying this to a real case. A client said this to me:

> I just don't know how to do this socialising thing. I find conversation so hard at social gatherings, I never know what to say. I was at a party this weekend, and someone said, 'You've been married for 30 years, what an amazing thing that is!' So I was thinking, what do I say next? Do I lie and be superficial and trivial and say yes, amazing, how great, or do I tell them the truth, which is sometimes my husband and I hate each other and it's been really hard and we've nearly broken up and we're in therapy at the moment about our relationship – do I say all of that? But I know my husband would be horrified if I said all of that. So how do I choose what to say?

I responded by explaining to her about titration. I said that you think about it droplet by droplet. First, say something to show you are receiving the droplet of conversation that the other person offered to you. This could be something neutral, non-committal, that just validates what they have said, like, 'Yes, well, it's certainly true that it's not so common these days to have a marriage of that length'.

At this point they know you are married, and for how long, so it's fine to comment on this in relation to them, asking whether they are married and for how long. Now that you both know these details about each other, this is a mutually accepted topic, and you could offer another droplet, that is authentic to your situation. You could say, 'Well, it's not always easy, is it?' And see how they respond to that droplet. They might say something like, 'Yeah it's really not always easy; it takes work', and then you have both come to that level, of mutually agreeing that it's not always easy. So you can go on from there, offering another droplet, or maybe they will.

If they don't respond to your droplet, showing an unfavourable reaction, then you know they don't want to go there, so you can go back to the previous level you had safely reached together, and ask something related but innocuous, like, 'How did you meet your husband/wife?' (That is usually a happy story for people, so it's taking them to something positive and comfortable for them.) Or you could offer the person an exit and change the subject, bringing up one of your ready-to-hand soothing topics (see the bullet points on soothing topics earlier in this chapter).

Similarly, if at any point they offer you a droplet you're not comfortable with, go back to a previous level or bring out one of your safe topics. The rule is to always keep it incremental and keep it reciprocal. This way, you can gradually ease into a deeper conversation – only if you both want to – and either of you can freely back off whenever you would like to.

This description of titration is also related to something else important in conversation, which is turn-taking. You offer a droplet and then wait for the other person's reaction. You do not keep pouring and pouring conversation at them. When taking turns, you can choose what your next droplet will be based on what you've already noticed about the person you're talking to, rather than simply imposing on them a droplet that was predetermined by you based on your interests or intentions and that has no reference to what you've observed of who the other person is or what state they're in.

During titration, how big or small the droplets are that are offered will be influenced by many factors such as culture, generational differences, kind of relationship, and context. For example, if you say you went to the doctor, a Peruvian would expect to hear all the graphic details, whereas an English person – especially in a workplace context – would assume you would want to keep this private, although between elderly English friends a sharing of graphic medical details often becomes part of regular conversation.

The point about titration is that you don't have to know all these things in advance, because you are being careful to offer contributions bit by bit and adjust what you say next according to the reaction you've received. If at any point there is a reaction that is more intense than mildly unfavourable – a bad reaction where the other person becomes overtly upset – you could salvage the conversation by doing a repair (follow the steps at the end of the section 'Skill no. 4: Expand', and also see the Chapter 7 boxout). Or, if you've had enough of talking to that person, or you don't like how it's going, or it seems clear the other person has had enough, then you can give up on that episode of communication. In this case, it is time to end the conversation.

Closing phase

Skill no. 6: End

For every conversation or episode/cycle of communication, there is a point when it comes to a close. This could happen because the goal of that conversation has been achieved – for example, in a workplace situation where you needed to report something to a person and that has been done. Or it could happen because time has run out – the time agreed in advance at which the conversation would end has been reached, or one of you has to leave to do something else. Or it could happen because either of you has lost interest in the conversation, or you are feeling great about it and want to leave on a high.

If talking on the phone or a video call, the end is the point when you hang up the phone or press the red 'leave' tab on the video call screen.

For conversations in person, it is the point when the two people involved physically move apart from each other, or if still physically in proximity, they direct their attention elsewhere – to another person, a film, a book, or whatever.

A conversation ideally ends with some mutually offered closing words. But it might not always be mutual – a conversation could end because one person hangs up on the other, or walks out, or you've been lying in bed together talking and one person falls asleep.

A good way to close a conversation is to start by naming that it is time to end. If you want to leave the conversation, own that; don't try to project it onto the other person. So, don't say, 'I should leave you to get on with other things now'. Instead, say, 'I need to go and get on with other things now'. Then you can say something (authentic) about how you feel about ending the conversation, giving away information for free ('I really enjoyed that', 'I wish we had more time', 'I'm sorry we're having to end on this difficult note', or 'I'd like to arrange another call/date/meeting – would you like that?') Show appreciation, even if it was difficult ('Thanks for the conversation' or 'I'm glad we had a chance to talk'), and say goodbye, or 'bye for now'.

After a conversation or communication cycle has ended, and before the next one begins

Skill no. 7: Reflect

After you have completed a conversation or cycle of communication, you'll be left with various impressions of the experience. These include the content of what was said and the process of how the interaction went. You're likely to have visual memories – images of how the other person looked and the surroundings while you talked – and auditory memories of the words that were spoken and how the voices sounded plus other associated sounds like perhaps background music that was playing. You'll be feeling something according to how the conversation went – perhaps satisfied, frustrated, neutral, joyful, angry. You could have felt different things at different points of the conversation. How do you make best sense of all these impressions?

You reflect.

It is typical to say we learn from experience, and this is true, but we learn a whole lot more from experience if, following the experience, we engage in deliberate reflection on it. Reflecting means thinking, or speaking, or writing, or drawing, in a way that involves mulling over an experience and noticing different elements of it and their effects, processing this, asking yourself questions about it, relating it to other things you know, filing away learnings from it, and making notes (physical or mental) for what more you'd like to find out in relation to it or what you'd like to do next time. By doing this you give yourself the best chance of improving the way you participate in next situations that are similar and of making sure you avoid repeating previous mistakes. Reflection is like digestion after eating: you're digesting what has been taken in, to derive maximum nutrition from it.

Reflection can relate primarily to a personal or professional context, although professional situations always also include a personal element. You can reflect on your own, in solitude and privacy. You can be reflecting while walking the dog, or writing in a journal, or drawing yourself a mind-map that captures the experience and related thoughts. Or you can reflect in conversation with someone else. Formalised ways of reflecting include attending a session of coaching, psychotherapy, or supervision in which a trained professional facilitates you to reflect. This can be done one-to-one or with more than one person.

For many years I ran Reflective Practice groups in organisations which involved conducting a once-a-month session of 90 minutes in which a team of staff and/ or management would step out of their busy day to reflect on their experiences at work. I would take them through the Gibbs Reflective Cycle,[12] which would begin with me inviting them to describe an incident at work. What happened?

In the next stage, I would invite them to describe their personal experience of what happened. What were they thinking and feeling? This was the stage I found people had most difficulty engaging with. Most often they would want to go from describing what happened straight to suggesting actions for how to manage this better if it arose again. In operational situations at work, like in team meetings, people typically go straight from naming an incident to working out what action to take in relation to it.

Reflection is different from action. It is about pausing to mull over and process something *before* considering action. In Reflective Practice sessions I would regularly have to gently bring the team back to sharing their personal responses to situations, reminding them this was a safe and confidential space where there would be no judgement on their thoughts and feelings. It was often this stage of reflection – the one that people would most readily skip – that they would later tell me was the one they found to be most powerful. In anonymous questionnaires I collected to evaluate the Reflective Practice sessions, what participants most often listed as most helpful was having their feelings validated rather than just being told what to do, discovering that other staff members were having similar experiences, and also learning from differences in how others in the team handled similar situations.

Following the stage of expressing and hearing thoughts and feelings, we would engage in the next stages of reflection: evaluating what was good and bad about the experience, analysing what sense could be made of it, and concluding what else could have been done. Only then comes action: if it arose again, what would you do? These are stages you can also go through when you reflect on your own experiences.

Using the seven IT'S BETTER essential communication skills

You can think of the seven skills as seven steps in a conversation, which can all be used, and in sequence, or you can use only the ones that the situation allows for, whichever one helps at whichever point. You can go back and forth between skills, using different ones repeatedly throughout the course of a conversation.

Because the reflect skill is something you can do at the end of a conversation, but also before a new conversation begins, the reflect skill can be seen as step 7 in a cycle of communication or also step zero.

Now that we have reached the end of this whole chapter which presented the seven essential skills, would you like to try out this skill of reflection right now? You can reflect on what your experience has been in reading this chapter. What has stood out most for you in reading about the seven essential skills? What feelings have been stirred up in you? What thoughts are forming for you? What action would you like to take in relation to this?

Do try this at home – Chapter 4 boxout

To be a good conversationalist it is vital that you become a good listener. Active listening involves not just passively letting a person's speech roll over you but incorporating the following pointers.

How to listen

- **Pay close attention to the other person**. Notice and be responsive to what they're saying and also how they're saying it – tone of voice, body posture, facial expression.
- **Show you are interested.** Use a body posture that opens yourself to the other person (turn towards them, don't hug folded arms against yourself that places a barrier between you and them). Give non-verbal encouragers (face the person, make eye contact, give nods and smiles) and verbal encouragers (say things like 'Mmm', 'Uh-uh', 'I'd love to hear more about . . . [name something specific]', and ask open questions like, 'How did you feel about that?', 'What happened next?').
- **Avoid interrupting.** Give the speaker the respect of waiting until they've finished before you take your turn to speak. (See the following game for practising this.)
- **Demonstrate that you've heard them**. A good way to show you've been actively listening is to begin your response by saying something that first 'receives' what the person said before you add your own new contribution to what they said. Show that you are letting what they have said 'land' with you, and you are validating that, before you add to it. You can say something as simple as, 'I see what you mean'. A more extensive way of doing

this is to paraphrase back to the person what they said. It could take this sort of form: 'So it sounds like you were really trying to . . . [whatever their intention was], and then when . . . [whatever happened], you felt . . . [whichever emotion is accurate].' This summarises what the person was telling you, with a focus on their personal engagement with it. This will make them feel you have really heard them, and not just the details of the situation but its personal meaning for them.

Here is a game you can play, which strengthens your capacity to control your own eagerness to speak, holding on to whatever is sparked for you by what the other person is saying until they stop speaking. This also ensures you genuinely respond to what the other person has said rather than simply imposing onto the conversation content of your own that is predetermined and not related to the state or situation of the other person.

Game instructions

1   One person (the speaker) begins talking, saying anything at all they would like to say.
2   Another person (the listener) must listen in silence until the speaker goes quiet.
3   When the speaker goes quiet, the listener must respond, but the first word of their response must begin with the last letter of the last word the speaker said.
4   Continue in this way, one person speaking and the other listening silently, with every response that is made following step 3, and see which person is first to get stuck or make a mistake.

I have played this game in presentations I have given to Mensa members, with audiences of adults and audiences of children, in different cities. I would have a queue of volunteers, with two playing the game, and as soon as one person got stuck, they would be out and the next person in line would take their place in the conversation. This produced a lot of amusement and laughter, and it was great fun seeing what inventive ways people came up with for keeping the conversation going.

Notes

1 ABC News (n.d.).
2 Isaacson (2011, p. 218).

3 Josias Murer II (Swiss, 1564–1630). *Orpheus Charming the Animals*, about 1600. Black ink and brown wash on paper, 22.9 × 18.6 cm (9 × 7 5/16 in.) The J. Paul Getty Museum, Los Angeles, 2001.22
4 Soanes et al. (2006).
5 guide.culturecrossing.net (n.d.)
6 Thomas and Inkson (2017).
7 Moyes (2010).
8 Moyes (2010, p. 71).
9 Personal conversation with Dr Laine Jaderberg, who has trained to work as a clown in contexts like supporting ill children in hospitals.
10 Bowlby (1958).
11 Schore (2017, p. 131).
12 See www.ed.ac.uk/reflection/reflectors-toolkit/reflecting-on-experience/gibbs-reflective-cycle

References

ABC News. (n.d.). Hillary and Bill: 'Immediate Attraction'. [online] *ABC News*. Available at: https://abcnews.go.com/2020/story?id=123702&page=1 [Accessed 25 June 2022].

guide.culturecrossing.net. (n.d.). *Culture Crossing* [online]. Available at: https://guide.culturecrossing.net/about_this_guide.php [Accessed 24 August 2022].

Isaacson, W. (2011). *Steve Jobs*. London: Little, Brown.

Moyes, J. (2010). *The Last Letter from Your Lover* (Reprinted 2021). London: Hodder.

Schore, A.N. (2017). Playing on the Right Side of the Brain. *American Journal of Play*, 9(2), pp. 105–142.

Soanes, C., Hawker, S. and Elliott, J. (eds) (2006). *Paperback Oxford English Dictionary*. Oxford: Oxford University Press.

Thomas, D.C. and Inkson, K.C. (2017). *Cultural Intelligence: Surviving and Thriving in the Global Village*. Oakland, CA: Berrett-Koehler Publishers.

5 Going deeper

Elaborating the top three of the seven skills

If you only remember three out of the seven essential skills from the previous chapter, these are the three I would choose as the most important ones: Soothe, Bridge, Titrate. These three skills still evoke the acronym of 'it's better', given that their initial letters – S, B, T – relate in sequence to the three syllables of 'it'*S B*et*T*er'. This chapter will discuss these three skills in more depth, with more examples, and particularly consider them in relation to extreme intelligence. But first, I want to address possible concerns related to implementing these skills.

Do I have to use these skills?

Of course you don't have to use any of these skills. It's your choice. I always tell my clients that I see this as being about simple cause and effect – any given behaviour will create consequences. I think it's helpful to understand what effect a form of behaviour will tend to have, because then you can choose whether you want that effect or not. I often find that clients are baffled by the difficulties they're experiencing with others, or they don't know how to get the reactions they hope for. Becoming more knowledgeable about communication skills, and more aware of what's going on for yourself and others, increases your chances of being effective in whatever kind of communication you're aiming for.

For example, after you've read the section on how to soothe and tried it out, you will know how to soothe, but do you want to soothe? Soothing makes a person more comfortable in your presence. There might be times when that's not what you want, maybe because you want to keep a competitive edge or exert authority or carry out necessary discipline rather than soften the interaction into a sense of acceptance or alliance. At Arsenal football team's home stadium they had all the knowledge and state-of-the-art resources available for how to build changing rooms that would make players feel confident and promote better communication among them. They created these conditions in their own team's changing rooms and then deliberately created the opposite conditions in the changing rooms of the visiting team who would be playing against them.

DOI:10.4324/9781003029106-8

You can always choose when it is appropriate or inappropriate to use a skill. For example, with titration, there are situations – like in a time-limited meeting or lecture – where you need to deliver your full message without the interruptions and distractions of giving others regular turns to contribute content of their own (their turn might have to wait until the scheduled Q&A). Also, when speaking to a group, you cannot be responsive to every individual in the group – while teaching, for example, one student might eagerly hang on your every word, while another in the same group has fallen asleep. When giving presentations online you cannot even see the faces of everyone in your audience, so you have to go ahead without the benefit of being able to make what you say more effective by adjusting it according to the reaction you're receiving.

Challenges in using these skills

Soothing, bridging, and titrating require generosity and take effort. Soothing to make someone feel comfortable with you is an act of generosity towards them. It takes effort to build a bridge with another person, to make yourself clearer to them, and to help facilitate them to draw nearer to you. Titrating involves disciplining yourself to hold back what you want to say and offering the other person the generosity of listening to them.

If you have not had your own needs met, it is hard to be generous to someone else. Individuals with extreme intelligence have often had a lifetime of experiencing their own needs not being acknowledged or addressed. Being disregarded in this way can leave them feeling ungenerous and impatient towards others and unwilling to make the effort (the 'Provoking' quadrant), or they might feel hopeless that making an effort is worth it (the 'Despairing' quadrant). I have come across several very high-IQ people who are particularly sensitive in public places to things like being accidentally bumped into or having their foot stepped on, getting instantly angry, and feeling they are being badly treated (rather than seeing it as an unpleasant but innocent and impersonal accident). I think they get especially aggrieved about this because it is symbolic of being disregarded, which is such a deep wound for them.

In the film *CODA*, which won the 2022 Oscar for best picture, the character Leo, who is deaf, rages against the hearing world, furious that he is meant to find ways to adjust to them rather than having them make the effort to adjust to him. Although frustrating, it is possible for an extremely intelligent person, when necessary, to slow down their speed or explain themselves in a simpler way. But for someone who does not have the necessary neurological features, it is impossible to speed up their pace or increase their complexity to the level of extreme intelligence, no matter how much they may want to or how hard they try. In this sense, it falls to the extremely intelligent person to take on the burden of adjustment.

You could call that unfair and be angry about that. You could also be grateful for the benefits of your extreme intelligence, and choose to radically accept it along with its burdens.

Marsha Linehan, founder of DBT (Dialectical Behaviour Therapy), describes 'radical acceptance' as choosing to turn your mind away from rejecting a reality that cannot be changed.[1] It is radical because it is so hard to accept something you find difficult or upsetting.

Radical acceptance does not mean you have to like or approve of that reality, nor that you become a passive victim of that reality, nor that you cannot do anything to work to change that reality. It simply means recognising that if you make your anger at that reality your focus, telling yourself it is unfair and shouldn't be that way, you can get stuck in that suffering and it can immobilise you. If, instead, you radically accept that it is that way, this is liberating: it frees you to concentrate on how best you can go forward from there. Of course, important changes throughout history have been initiated by revolutionaries who practice a radical *non*-acceptance of how things are. You always have to exercise your judgement about what is a reality that you can work to change, and what is one that you will accept. Either way, getting stuck in the suffering of being upset about the fact of a reality is purely debilitating. It is like the profound words of Reinhold Niebuhr's prayer: 'Grant me the serenity to accept the things I cannot change, courage to change the things I can, and wisdom to know the difference'.[2]

Such acceptance is easier for a person with extreme intelligence if the reality of this individual difference is named and validated for them, if compassion is shown towards them for how difficult it is living as a minority in a world that is not designed for them, and if they have at least one domain in their lives where they can interact with one or more others similar to themselves. I have found that this kind of acknowledgement immediately drains away a lot of the anger and isolation. This helps such individuals feel better about themselves and fuels them to be able to offer more generosity and effort when needed.

Developing and maintaining proficiency in a skill

Slowing down the way you interact with others and becoming more self-conscious about it rather than just going along robustly in the way you usually do can feel like you're making things worse for yourself interpersonally rather than better. I have had clients with extreme intelligence complain about how hard they found it to Bridge and how exhausting to Titrate, having to monitor others' responses and modulate themselves, saying how they long to just be themselves and let go without being afraid this will in some way cause harm (and we are culturally surrounded by the aphorism 'just be yourself', which is misleading: being yourself in terms of being authentic is to be encouraged, whereas being yourself in terms of behaving tactlessly or thoughtlessly is never going to go well).

My response to this is – who said it should be easy? Why is there an expectation that a skill worth having will be easy to acquire? Maybe neurotypical people find communication easier because those skills come more naturally to them or because the way they function is more similar to the majority of others. However, there are many other things that neurotypical people find much harder than the very high-IQ person does. A person with extreme intelligence can assimilate a lot of information, see patterns, come up with new ideas, and learn and master things quickly, all with much less effort than it takes for neurotypical people. So, there are advantages and disadvantages.

Because so much learning (of the intellectual kind) has been quick and easy for those with extreme intelligence, they can be surprised when any kind of learning is difficult or requires more time and effort. But bringing yourself to a more advanced level of skill in almost anything does take time and effort. For example, you might be able to play a range of pieces on the piano with some degree of comfort and competence. If, however, you want to develop your playing to a more advanced level, this will usually require breaking down the movements involved and becoming more self-conscious about them. You will have to watch exactly how each finger moves so you can train it to move a bit differently. While you're working to master a new level of technical skill, you are not making music; you're doing exercises. But once you apply your new level of skill to playing a piece, you will find you can play the piece much better and also tackle more advanced pieces. So overall your playing improves significantly.

Breaking communication down into different skills, becoming conscious of these and deliberately practising them, might feel awkward and unnatural, but soon you will get used to them, experience reinforcing rewards, and it will become second nature, so that eventually you will be employing them more unconsciously with good results. Learning anything new begins with being unconsciously incompetent, then moves to becoming consciously incompetent (which is the most difficult phase). This moves then to becoming consciously competent, and eventually to becoming unconsciously competent.[3]

Even once you become more unconsciously competent at a new skill, it requires ongoing effort to keep it in good shape. Musicians who stop practising soon find that the proficiency of their performance declines. Just staying physically healthy requires ongoing effort. Taking regular exercise might not always be what you feel like doing, but when you put in the effort, you get the immediate payoff of an exhilarating dose of endorphins and the longer-term payoff of a fitter, leaner, more supple body.

It's the same with interpersonal skills. They might take effort, but I've regularly heard people praise the positives of the connection they experience with others when they are managing to communicate effectively and it's going well, and how rewarding that process is, in addition to the longer-term rewards of building better relationships.

The Soothe skill: anticipating sensitivities in advance

Part of getting good at soothing involves beginning to anticipate what anxiety or sensitivity might be triggered in another person and working to quell it in advance. Remember from Chapter 1 that sensitivities relate to cues of safety versus danger. Safety is signalled when you are understood, accepted, and included. Danger is signalled when you are misunderstood, criticised, and excluded. It is helpful not to think of every person you communicate with as though they are a bullet-proof entity to whom you are machine-gunning your thoughts or directives. Instead, always think of the other person as being Shakespeare's snail, keeping in mind that if you hit a tender horn they will 'shrink backward' into their 'shelly cave with pain', 'long after fearing to creep forth again'.[4]

To implement this new mindset, you can scan your proposed communication in advance – or while delivering it – to check what cues it contains. If you want the communication to go well, you can deliberately choose to incorporate cues of safety and avoid cues of danger. Taking into account the individuality of the person involved, and what their specific triggers might be, can help you tailor your message even better to be suited to them. This is part of the preparation phase of a communication cycle. It applies to spoken and written communication.

With written communication you have much more time to plan what you say, plus the opportunity to edit it in advance of sending it. Applying the principles of soothing to written communication is a good way, therefore, to begin practising with them. I'll give an example of how you can do this when writing an email.

The Soothe skill: the principles of soothing applied in detail to writing an email

Two examples come to mind of emails I received that instantly stirred a negative reaction in me. One was from a Mensa member – a stranger to me – who sent me a diatribe about why he thought I should have used the word 'use' rather than 'utilise' in something I wrote, telling me all the reasons he didn't like the word 'utilise', and ending with 'there's a good girl'. I felt criticised and patronised, which are feelings that do not make you feel safe and inspired to communicate further. Another was an email from someone who had read one of my books. The very first line of the email was: 'You and I should talk'. There wasn't even an opening line addressing me. It felt presumptuous, and like I was being told what to do, without being given a choice ('Would you like to talk?'). It was such a bad start that I couldn't bring myself to reply.

When writing an email, you can first type up whatever you wish to say in draft, fast and uncensored, but I recommend making sure there is no recipient's address filled in while you do this so you cannot accidentally send it. Then, after you've written it, check over it and edit according to the following principles before filling in the recipient's address and sending it (it's a bit of a long list, but these things do become habit after you've tried them a few times):

- *Have you started with something courteous?* Even just a few words that show a recognition of who the recipient is and what they might be experiencing. This will help make them more receptive to your message.

- *Have you stated your message clearly?* This includes making it clear whether you want something from the other person, and if so, what it is. 'I am writing to . . . so could you please let me have the following two items (and number them)'. Or 'Further to . . . I need to understand . . . so could you please let me have the answer to the following question . . .' Where possible, limit an email to dealing with one main point. You can also Titrate by email: send one email containing one main point, and hold back your next point until you have seen what reaction you receive.
- *Is anything open to misinterpretation?* Edit to remove ambiguity.
- *Can you be more concise?* Check for content that is not directly relevant, and which adds no value (e.g. it is repetitive, or unnecessary for the current topic), and eliminate.
- *Can you rephrase to state something more tentatively?* Rather than stating things categorically, it is helpful to incorporate humility, showing recognition that there might be other relevant information or perspectives that you aren't aware of.
- *Can you add something that shows respect for the other person?* Imagine the recipient as someone who is valuable, with a lot of things taking up their time and attention, and phrase what you say in ways that are not demanding. Say things like 'When you have a chance I would be grateful if you could . . .'
- *Is there anything that could make the recipient feel criticised?* Remove or reword, even if it's subtle. At the end of a race in which formula one driver Charles Leclerc's performance was compromised by a technical malfunction that was the responsibility of his supporting engineering team, he was interviewed on camera. Instead of saying, 'We will have to find out what went wrong with the tyres', he said, 'We will have to find out what went on with the tyres'.
- *Is there anything that could make the recipient's interests, value, or autonomy, from their perspective, appear to be being disregarded?* If so, reword it.
- *Can you think of something (genuine) that positively acknowledges the recipient's interests, value, or autonomy?* If so, add it.
- *Are you aware of any obvious assumption or emotion you could be stirring up, that you can address in advance?* If so, name it, and work to lay it to rest in advance. For example, 'I think you might worry this proposal is too daunting. Please know I am quite relaxed about timescale and I'm happy to discuss how we can break it down into stages'. If they have been late replying to something, let them know, in advance, that you will be welcoming of their response: 'I'll be really pleased to hear from you'. This soothes them from a fear that a late response could elicit anger from you, which could be what is holding them back from responding.
- *Can you add more courtesy?* Have you said please where you can, and thank you where you can?
- *Have you allowed a margin for human error in what you've said?* Avoid communicating that you expect perfection, either from others or from yourself.

- *Is there any reference to a previous issue that was difficult, which you can omit?* No matter what difficult thing might have happened before, rather than looking backwards, stay focused on the current issue and demonstrate a willingness to go forward in a positive way. This includes avoiding saying things like 'as I have told you before', or 'you haven't responded yet'. This follows the general principle of not pointing out another person's mistakes or failings.
- *Is there any presumptuousness you can edit out?* For example, don't thank a person for doing something you want them to do if they haven't yet explicitly agreed to do it. ('Will you kindly step in and do that session? Many thanks!') And don't add 'kindly', or smiley faces, simply as a tool to aid manipulation or soften coercion. People will see through this and it won't go down well.

I recommend applying these same principles in spoken communication also. Talking is a communication medium that is more instant and less controllable, but also at least does not provide a physical record that cannot be deleted.

The Bridge skill: empathy and mentalisation

'Empathy' and 'mentalisation' are terms that relate to significant bodies of research and practice in psychology and psychotherapy, and which are directly relevant to what I am calling the Bridge skill. Empathy involves two components: a cognitive drive to understand what another is thinking and feeling, and an affective drive to respond appropriately to their emotional state. Mentalisation is 'mind-mindedness',[5] which means recognising that other people have minds, that what is going on in people's minds informs their behaviour, and that other people's minds are different from your own.

Here is an example. My builder asks me, 'What new doors do you want?' I say, 'Please just get wooden doors with frosted glass.' He says, 'Can you maybe go online and order them yourself because I don't actually know what you want?' I'm thinking, how can he not know what I want when I've already told him? And it's so simple – all I want is a wooden door with glass in it that lets the light through but is frosted for privacy. I feel he is being unhelpful, trying to get me to do something that is part of his job, when I am way too busy, and this annoys me.

When I go online, I discover there are masses of different wooden doors with frosted glass. Patterned frosting or plain frosting, different numbers of wooden panels in proportion to different sizes of glass, and different kinds of wood – oak, pine, mahogany. And then the wood could be pre-finished or raw. And there are different thicknesses of door, and different handle options. Brass? Chrome? Round handle or lever handle? In my mind 'wooden door with frosted glass' was so simple, but in his mind, because he knows the industry much better than I do, he knew it was much more complicated. He wasn't being unhelpful. He was realising that he could easily have bought and installed a door I would not have liked, because it might not have matched whatever picture I had in my mind.

Mentalisation is about stepping back from an immediate reaction to someone's behaviour and being *curious* about what made them behave that way. It involves learning to understand your own mental state so you can describe it rather than just act on it. It involves learning to imagine what others might be thinking and feeling rather than simply reacting to their behaviour. Mentalisation has been described as being able to see yourself from the outside and see others from the inside.[6]

When you see yourself from the outside, you are thinking about how another person sees you, and what is missing from what they know about you. This helps you be alert to what information about yourself you can offer them (for free) that will build a bridge between what you know about your situation and what they know about it.

Similarly, when you see another person from the inside, this means you are thinking about what might be going on for them that you don't know about which is affecting their behaviour. This helps you formulate things you can say to them or ask them that will help build a bridge that enables you to draw nearer to each other.

Empathy is often described as 'putting yourself in the other person's shoes'. But a crucial insight is that it's not about putting yourself in the other person's shoes, as though *you* are in their situation and experiencing it from what your own perspective would be if you were in their situation. It's about working to understand what *their* perspective would be within that situation, how *their* mind (different from yours) manages within that situation they are in. Otherwise you're operating by projection: projecting who you are onto their situation, rather than empathising with who they are. Being able to operate in a way that takes the other person's perspective into account is also referred to as 'perspective taking'.

Here is an easy way to demonstrate this difference. Imagine you hear that someone has just arrived for the first time at Machu Picchu. Perhaps you immediately imagine what feelings of awe and exhilaration they'll be experiencing as they stand before this iconic ancient citadel perched on a very high mountain ridge, with panoramic views, because this is how you would feel if you were standing there, 'in their shoes'. But now, if you learnt that this person is blind, how would that affect what you had imagined?

The Bridge skill: the starting point

Sometimes someone will say or do something that shocks you with how different it is from what you think or what you would do. At a moment like that, it is as though that person – even if you are closely related to them – has become alien to you, a distance away from you on the bridge, in fog. In that situation, people often expend time and energy having a big reaction about how could that person think or do that? So they are spending time and energy being shocked that the other person has a mind different from their own.

In that situation, you can think of the other person's thinking and behaviour as being their starting point on the bridge. There is not much use going on about how terrible their starting point is, from your perspective, or wishing their starting point was different or thinking how much better things could be if there was a different starting point. The fact is that their starting point is what it is.

Instead of spending time and energy reacting to what that person's starting point is, you can better invest time and energy into working out where to go from that starting point onwards. If you can radically accept and respect that this is what their starting point is, and that they will have good reasons for having arrived at that point – just like your own starting point in any situation comes from your own good reasons – then you can be curious about their starting point, learn more about it to better understand it, and work out what is needed to move from there towards where you want to go next, whether that is going to be together with that person or separately from them.

The Bridge skill: who covers the most distance

For two people to better understand each other, ideally both of them would be making efforts to build a bridge that helps them move nearer and become clearer to each other. When this happens, each person is covering a similar distance over that bridge to meet in the middle.

But say, for example, you have read this book which has equipped you with the Bridge skill, but the other person hasn't read it. If they have no awareness of how to Bridge, then for the two of you to better understand each other would require you to do more of the work to build that bridge. You might think that's unfair, that you're putting in more of the work. But if they are not equipped, or not yet equipped, to help with that work, then the only way things will improve between you is if you radically accept that you are the one who will have to cover more of the distance to meet with them and that this meeting might only be possible closer to their end of the bridge.

When there are large differences between people, the bridge-building takes more effort and might not be viable for closer or more long-term relationships. It is easier to make such efforts when they are needed if you balance this out with seeking others to regularly spend time with or work with who are similar to yourself in functioning and/or in level of communication skill. Be willing to find kindred spirits in unexpected ways or places. Many people with extreme intelligence have not had traditional educations and are not living lifestyles that easily give outward signs of their abilities, so you might not realise how much they have to offer. Also, when you have become used to feeling like an outsider, you might have developed a habit of looking at others with the expectation that you and they will not understand each other, and this will blinker you to similarities that exist between you and others.

The Bridge skill: client example

An extremely intelligent client complained to me about how she was a complete outsider at work, and couldn't fit in with her colleagues at all. 'They talk about such trivial things', she said, 'like clothes, and I can't join in, I have nothing to say about that and I'm not interested'.

I said, 'But you also wear clothes? You have to go and buy clothes for yourself?'

'Yes', she admitted. 'That's true.'

We talked more. I said, 'It sounds like you're saying you feel you can only have conversations with people who discuss things you feel are serious, like politics.'

She said, 'It's not that I only want to talk about serious things or only ever have serious things on my mind – my mind is filled with all sorts of silly and trivial things, so it's not as though I'm only concerned with serious things. With my friends, I do talk about clothes.'

I said, 'So, what makes the difference between people who you do talk about silly things with, and those with whom you feel you can't?'

She said, 'My friends are people I know I can talk about important things with, and so as an extension of that or part of that, we can also talk about silly things together. But other people who I see as not being able to talk about serious things, I don't want to involve myself in talking with them about silly things.'

'How do you know that those girls at the office can only talk about trivial things and not ones you consider important?'

'Because I've never heard them talk about anything more important; they're always talking about clothes.'

'Have you tried raising the topic yourself, about something more important?'

'No', she said.

'Okay. You've not initiated talking about something more serious, so you don't know whether they would be able to talk about that or be interested or not.'

'Well, there was one time when I asked them whether they knew why there was a tube strike and they didn't, they didn't know anything about it!'

'But in that situation, you were asking them if they knew the reason, because you yourself didn't know the reason?'

'Oh yeah . . .'

All people will at times not know something. All people will at times have to deal with something trivial, and at times with something important. If you recognise this, you can be willing to see the ways in which you and others are similar to each other.

This client was approaching her colleagues with the assumption that they were completely different from her, and somehow worse than herself, from the stance of 'I'm OK, you're not OK'. She was criticising their conversation as trivial, ignoring the fact that her own conversation (with her friends) could be equally trivial.

There is the issue here of whether she would want to build a bridge between herself and her colleagues. If your identity has become based on being different and set apart from others, you might feel you are relinquishing your uniqueness if you show similarity with others or make it easier for them to understand you. Also, if you feel wounded that others seem to be excluding you, if you don't know the Bridge skill or don't want to put in the effort of using that skill, then (like Mr. B in Chapter 2) you could instead tell yourself they are not worth associating with (the defence of rationalisation) or that you like being set apart from them (the defence of reaction formation). (See Chapter 2 for a recap on these defences.)

The Titrate skill: interruption versus waiting your turn

Very high-IQ people can find it hard to wait their turn in conversation. One reason is that they have a lot going on in their minds and strong reactions, so it's hard to suppress something they feel is bursting from them to be said. Another reason is that their minds work fast and they can often see where the other person's sentence is going, or even where their whole idea is going, and so instead of waiting for it to unfold at the other person's pace, they get impatient and want to start responding.

Where the participants in a conversation know each other well and are happy to accept interruptions of this kind, that's a perfectly good – and very enjoyable – conversational style for both of them. Often, though, a person will experience it as rude if you interrupt their flow. This can feel like a microaggression – as though you're bulldozing them – which will put the other person into a state of defence rather than a state of safety.

With someone you don't know well, be careful to check this out. Watch for favourable versus unfavourable reactions (as described in Chapter 4, in the section on Skill no. 5). If their reaction shows they did not appreciate your interruption, instead of just throttling on, stop and acknowledge this. You can say something like, 'Oh dear, I'm sorry, I notice I just interrupted you. I thought I knew what you were going to say and I was eager to respond'. (Give away information for free.) 'But maybe I got it wrong.' (Be humble.)

On the other hand, a favourable reaction can show that the person is thrilled you have really 'got' what they were saying, and so fast, and they might happily stop and let you speak, then maybe even interrupt you. (Let them! It's your turn to stop.) In this way you can keep bouncing off each other, the conversation speeding up and getting more intense with increasing signs of mutual enjoyment.

Sometimes the way someone is experiencing something is easy to read from their reaction, but sometimes a person can be harder to read (or the person doing the reading finds this harder to do). In such a case, you can more explicitly ask for feedback.

The Titrate skill: receiving and giving feedback

In a conversation, the other person might expect that you are able to intuit what they're feeling or wanting, and if you don't, they might see you as insensitive. If you are aware you don't intuit these things easily, it can be very helpful to let others know that you would really appreciate it if they told you more explicitly what they are thinking/feeling/wanting.

You can say something like, 'I don't know if it's ever like this for you, but I'm not always good at reading a situation. Can I check what you're thinking/feeling/wanting right now?' By beginning with 'I don't know if it's ever like this for you . . .' you are recognising that all people sometimes experience these things, which demonstrates a stance of 'I'm OK, you're OK'. There is no need to depict yourself as 'I'm not OK' because of what you are experiencing. By beginning in this way, you are making that experience sound like an ordinary human experience. And you are inviting the other person to find similarities between you, by recalling to their own mind occasions on which they have experienced the same thing.

Finding out from others how they are experiencing an interaction with you (receiving feedback) and letting them know how you are experiencing them (giving feedback) are invaluable for improving communication. It is helpful to facilitate these behaviours but preferably without even using the term 'feedback'. This is because we live in a culture where we are constantly being asked to give feedback almost anytime we buy anything or use any kind of service, so we might be really sick of the concept of feedback.

You can generate feedback in an organic-feeling way by saying things like, 'I know I can tend to go too fast sometimes – please tell me if you want me to slow down'. Or you can check the other person is still with you, by asking questions like, 'Is this making sense to you?' 'What do you think about that?', or 'I've been told I sometimes leave out steps when I'm explaining something, which I usually don't even realise. So please let me know if I can explain this better?' This shows that you expect things won't always go smoothly, that this is something you are fine with hearing about, and that you would like to modulate your communication according to their reaction.

People often won't give explicit feedback on how they're experiencing you unless you tell them you would welcome it. This is usually because they would be afraid you might have a bad reaction, so they avoid it. If you do ask for feedback, let them know in advance that you will have a calm reaction (in other words, soothe them), so that they feel safe to do this. And then if they do give you honest feedback, ensure you follow through and do stay calm.

Receiving feedback might well stir up instant difficult feelings in you. Typical ways of reacting when you feel someone is suggesting you could do something better is to go through the following three stages[7]:

1   'Fuck you.'
2   'I suck.'
3   'Okay, what?'

Often people get stuck in one of the first two stages, and don't even get to the third stage, which is the one in which they become more receptive to understanding what the feedback means for them. You can see how 'Fuck you' is the fight reaction, and 'I suck' is the flight or freeze reaction, perceiving a threat. 'Okay, what?' becomes possible when you're feeling safe.

If you receive feedback and find yourself in the first two phases, engage your self-soothing skills for helping to return yourself to a state of safety. Begin, always, with breathing. Here are some pointers for receiving feedback:

- *Listen to the feedback.* Rather than interrupting and rejecting or arguing with the feedback, hear the person out. Remind yourself it is only that person's own perspective. Afterwards you can reflect on what it means for you.
- *Ask for any clarification needed.* Ensure you have understood, and are not misinterpreting, their message.
- *Check whether there's anything else relevant they'd like to say.* It's better to hear all there is rather than have someone hide things because you've reacted badly.
- *Be courteous.* Thank them for the feedback, and say you will give it some thought.
- *Then in your own space and time, reflect on it.* Check it out with others if possible, to maintain a balanced view. Decide what you think of it, and if, and how, you might want to use it – it's your choice.

If you are in a conversation where you feel the urge to give the other person any feedback that is not purely positive, never just blurt it out. First, give them a choice. Ask them whether they would like to hear some feedback from you. If they consent, then in whatever you say, make clear that it's only your own perspective and that they are free to make of it whatever they wish.

By encouraging others to let you know how they're experiencing things, you're encouraging their freedom to express themselves and you are greeting their expressiveness with acceptance. This feels good for a person and makes them feel good about you. (This is what moves people towards the 'Thriving' quadrant.)

Do try this at home – Chapter 5 boxout

We can be much freer in how we interact with others if we are not afraid of feelings – either the feelings others provoke in ourselves or the feelings we might provoke in others. If you have found emotions problematic and have become disconnected from them, this is how you can begin to reconnect.

How to not be afraid of feelings

- **Whenever you feel something intense – breathe.** Follow the instructions on 'How to Breathe' in the Chapter 1 boxout.
- **Whatever you are feeling, know that it is temporary.** It will pass. Every kind of feeling – bad ones and also good ones – will last for about 20 minutes. It is like a wave that gathers, peaks in intensity, then subsides. Don't be afraid of the wave – ride the wave. Breathe through it, noticing how it comes and then goes.
- **Know that you don't have to do anything.** It is important to separate feelings and thoughts from actions – you can feel something or think something and simply let it be, waiting it out. It is best *not* to do anything at the height of an intense wave of feeling – murder someone, marry someone – as you might regret it later. Focus on identifying and describing what you are feeling (to yourself and maybe someone else), rather than acting on it. Later, when the most intense peak of feeling has passed, you can decide what to do.
- **Learn about feelings.** Even start by looking at emojis to see which one best expresses how you feel, then put a word or words to it. Resources like Tiffany Watt Smith's *The Book of Human Emotions* (2016) and Plutchik's Wheel of emotions (1982, 2019) – see Figure 5.1 – can help you find names for different feelings and learn to understand how feelings work and relate to each other. By tracing the lines that link the different emotions in this image, you can find, for example, that anger + joy = pride.
- **Remember that everything feels worse when you are tired/hungry/ill.** When something feels overwhelming, ensure you're doing what you can to stay well, rested, fed, and hydrated. The English are not so crazy to greet any difficulty with first making a cup of tea. A hot drink can be soothing. And however bad today seems, remind yourself that you get a new day tomorrow to work at it again.
- **Self-soothe.** Find methods that work for you. Breathing is the first and most important method of soothing yourself any time you become overwhelmed by an intense feeling. But there are many other methods. For example: doing physical exercise, immersing your face in a basin of iced water, immersing your body in a hot bath, using fragrant oils/candles, practising mindfulness/meditation, using visualisation, journaling, talking to friends, therapy, reading/listening to/watching something you enjoy that's entertaining or educational, going out into nature, or cooking a meal.
- **Exercise your psychic muscles for increased fitness.** The more you allow yourself to experience and manage different feelings, the

more familiar you will become with feelings, the less worried you'll be by them, the more ease you will have in social interactions and in life in general, and the more general contentment and fulfilment you will experience.

- **Welcome feelings into your life.** Be welcoming towards feelings. Approach them with curiosity – what does it mean that I/you are feeling this right now? In this way you can mine them for valuable data.
- **Value feelings as your built-in compass.** Feelings provide you with direction towards what matters to you and away from what is negative for you.
- **But remember feelings are not everything.** Remember from Chapter 1 about how Emotion mind needs to be integrated with Reason mind to create Wise mind.

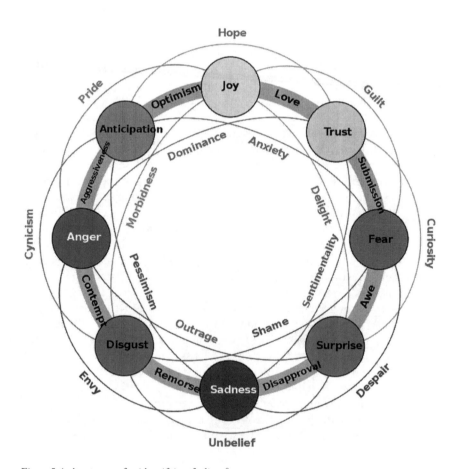

Figure 5.1 A resource for identifying feelings[8]

Notes

1 Linehan (2015).
2 See Kaplan (2002), which attributes the prayer to Niebuhr in 1943.
3 Du Plock and Barber (2015).
4 Shakespeare, W. *Venus and Adonis*, 1031–6.
5 Fonagy (2006).
6 Fonagy (2006).
7 Attributed to Bradley Whitford, cited in Bintliff (2022).
8 Plutchik's Dyads.

References

Bartlett, J. (2002). Reinhold Niebuhr (1892–1971). In J. Kaplan (ed) *Bartlett's Familiar Quotations* (17th ed.). New York: Little, Brown and Company, p. 735.

Bintliff, E. (2022). Feedback: Why Do We Find It So Hard to Take? *FT Weekend Magazine*, 23/24 July, pp. 24–31.

Du Plock, S. and Barber, P. (2015). Facilitating High Achievers to Tell Their Stories of Professional Entrepreneurialism: Lessons from the Doctorate in Psychotherapy by Professional Studies. In S. Goss and C. Stevens (eds) *Making Research Matter*. London: Routledge, pp. 25–34.

Kaplan, J. (ed.) (2002). Reinhold Niebuhr (1892–1971). In *Bartlett's Familiar Quotations* (17th ed.), p. 735. New York: Little, Brown and Company.

Linehan, M.M. (2015). *DBT Skills Training Manual* (2nd ed.). New York: The Guilford Press.

Plutchik, R. (1982). A Psychoevolutionary Theory of Emotions. *Social Science Information*, 21, pp. 529–553. doi:10.1177/053901882021004003.

Plutchik's Dyads. (2019). Infographic by ChaoticBrain, *Wikimedia Commons*. Available at: https://commons.wikimedia.org/wiki/File:Plutchik_Dyads.svg

Watt Smith, T. (2016). *The Book of Human Emotions: An Encyclopedia of Feeling from Anger to Wanderlust*. London: Profile Books Ltd.

Part III
Practice
How to have better conversations

6 General conversation (including small talk)

Czech novelist Milan Kundera likened conversation to a battle, the aim of which is to occupy the other person's ear.[1] He described people as just waiting for a chance to get attention for themselves, saying, 'That's just like me, I . . .' at the first opportunity they get, as a tenuous link towards gaining dominance of the conversation. Such behaviour would be my idea of fruitless conversation.

In fruitless conversation, the participants do not engage in active listening nor allow safe surprises to emerge, but instead use the conversation to impose on the other person their own pre-existing ideas and preoccupations. Three possible outcomes of such conversation are as follows:

1 Nothing worthwhile (including feel-good hormones) emerges for anyone.
2 Something that was needed or hoped for is not achieved.
3 It makes one or more person upset or even seriously aggrieved.

These disappointing outcomes can happen in any context of conversation. But what I repeatedly hear from individuals with extreme intelligence is that the context they find most difficult, is general conversation in which there is no task focus or clear agenda, such as a gathering that is just for socialising, and particularly when the type of interaction called 'small talk' is involved. This chapter looks at some general principles for avoiding undesirable conversational outcomes, then focuses on small talk in particular.

Timing

My late mother was right about almost everything. But although she had great wisdom and an uncanny prescience, on several occasions she caused (unintended) offence. This is because she was not always careful about timing. For example, when her friend Alice's[2] elderly husband had a first hospitalisation, she told Alice it was best that he be put in a nursing home and that Alice shouldn't feel bad about this.

Ultimately the husband might well have needed nursing home care, and at such a point the wife's inevitable feelings of guilt could have been helped by having a friend sanction this course of action. But Alice wasn't there yet. Alice

DOI: 10.4324/9781003029106-10

was fully absorbed with just managing this first hospitalisation, whereas my mother was fast-forwarding to the future and speaking about things her friend was nowhere near ready for considering. Even if my mother was right, she said it too soon, so her friend was horrified and upset, rather than grateful for the support. This is like the Greek mythological character Cassandra. She could see far ahead, and she was right, but no one believed her, and she was vilified for saying what she saw.

Individuals with extreme intelligence often look far ahead of the current moment. To work out whether the timing is right for saying what you can see lying ahead, it is important to employ the Bridge skill. Before saying what's on your mind, first find out what state the other person is in – check what they are feeling and how they are seeing things. And then build a bridge between where they are at and what you're saying.

Timing relates to the Tune skill. Remembering the orchestra analogy from Chapter 4, tuning is the necessary starting point before playing but timing is crucial throughout musical performance if the instruments are to remain in harmony. Timing is important in terms of the process of the conversation ('Is this a good time to talk?') and the content of the conversation ('Is this a good time to raise this particular subject?') When thinking about timing in a conversation, it's better if all seven of the IT'S BETTER essential communication skills are used.

I – Begin with 'I' – 'I will take responsibility for how I make this communication.'

T – *Tune* in to the other person to check whether it's a good time to talk. Are they relaxed? Or preoccupied? Is there enough time to adequately discuss the subject? Is that subject something they are likely to be receptive to now? Sometimes an idea will be better received if you hold on to it and wait for a good time to raise it rather than blurting it out the minute you first have the idea.

S – *Soothe* to help prepare a person to be receptive to your message. If you anticipate that what you want to say could stir difficult feelings for them, say this in advance. For example, 'I think you might not be happy about this, but I'd really like to work with you to find a good solution'.

B – *Bridge*. Think about how the other person might receive what you're planning to say. What can you say that builds a bridge between their position and what you'd like to say? For example, do they know enough about the issue at hand? Test with open questions. If not, offer information that helps introduce them – from their perspective – to what you want to say.

E – *Expand* beyond this one conversation right now. What do you know about this person's context – family situation, education, culture, generation – that you can take into account in the way you communicate with them?

TT – *Titrate.* Begin with part of what you mean to say and check the reaction first before going ahead full throttle with the whole content.

E – *End* the conversation in a courteous way, regardless of how it went.

R – *Reflect* on how that went. Was that the best timing for that subject? Learn from how this went so that when next you want to raise something, you can reflect in advance on how you can best approach it.

It is crucial for success in communication that you bring the other person along with you. For example, if there is a course of action you want to recommend, it should be something the other person is ready for, and can own, rather than feel has been imposed on them, and especially not imposed on them prematurely. That makes all the difference as to whether your recommendation can be accepted or whether you, as the communicator of it, get punished for it. This is a bit like 'shooting the messenger' – be careful not to be shot.

In various situations, including teaching and psychotherapy, there is the option of telling the other person what you already know, or facilitating them to discover it for themselves. The latter takes patience, which can be hard, especially for very high-IQ people who often have a strong urge to immediately say what they're thinking. But facilitating someone to discover for themselves is much more effective. Referring to this principle, psychoanalyst D. W. Winnicott wrote, 'If only we can wait, the patient arrives at understanding creatively and with immense joy, and I now enjoy this joy more than I used to enjoy the sense of having been clever'.[3]

Preserving the relationship

When dealing with how, or whether, to express thoughts you have during a conversation, a helpful principle to apply is 'preserve the relationship'. Instead of simply saying what you are seeing or thinking in the moment, consider what impact it might have on your relationship with that person if you were to say that thing at that moment. In this sense, you are employing the principle of 'playing the long game' (see Chapter 3), because instead of seeing every little interaction as something you have to, for example, be right about, you are letting go of that towards thinking about the longer-term aims of the well-being of a relationship.

In the practice of psychotherapy we call the relationship with the client the 'working alliance'. If you cannot keep a viable working alliance intact, the client will not be receptive to anything you say, and will not have any incentive to persevere with working with you through difficult conversations, so you won't be able to achieve anything. Research on what builds a good working alliance emphasises three main characteristics: acceptance, genuineness, and empathy.[4] These are the same three characteristics that Carl Rogers, a pioneer in the field of counselling, emphasised as providing the 'core conditions' that would enable a person to flourish.[5]

If things get tough in a conversation, you can name the relationship, say that you value it, and that it is your intent to preserve it. This involves taking a step outside of the content of the current conversation and making a comment on the process. For example,

> I know we are struggling with this topic of finances [or whatever the topic is] right now, and that we both want to resolve it [refer to both of you being together in it, rather than one against the other]. However we eventually do resolve it [show confidence that you will be able to resolve it], I want you to know I really care about our relationship – you are more important to me than any particular arrangements we make.

Criticism

Related to the subject of pointing out to others what you already know or can see lying ahead is that very high-IQ people often seem to delight in pointing out other people's mistakes, as though they have to prove their worth by showing that they can see what others have missed. But that is very likely to just make the other person fight or flee.

When you feel the urge to say something corrective or critical, it is helpful to pause before saying anything and first consider whether saying it is really necessary. Is it important? Will it be important beyond the current moment? If not, there's no need to say it. If it is important, can you say it in a way that will preserve, rather than damage, your relationship with that person?

If you see faults but don't say them, this is not you being fake or inauthentic; it is simply you making a choice to serve the bigger purpose of overall enhancing the relationship rather than parading whatever faults you see just because you can see them. People generally don't welcome unsolicited advice or want to feel that you're trying to fix them. They won't appreciate having it pointed out that they're not doing something as well as you know how to do it. It might be that you do know how to do it better, but is it worth pointing this out if it damages your relationship with that person?

When it is the other way around, and you are the person on the receiving end of criticism, you might yourself go straight into fight or flight. Individuals with extreme intelligence have high sensitivity and can experience another person's comments with more intensity than the other person intended. An example is a text exchange where Kim asked Marie[6] a question about why she'd done something a certain way, and Marie responded with, 'I feel like I've been slapped'. This was a very strong reaction. Marie was being authentic in expressing how she experienced Kim's question, but she was not being skilful. Her choice of words implied that Kim had done something aggressive, when Kim's question could be seen as innocuous. Being accused of aggression will instantly put Kim in a state of defence rather than a state of safety.

If you find yourself having a strong reaction, breathe, pause, and think about whether it is as severe as you initially experienced it as being. Is it possible to find a more benign interpretation of what just happened? You might feel like you've been plunged into deep water that will drown you and you're fighting for your life, but could you instead see it as a muddy puddle you have stepped into, which is unwelcome to have stepped into, but which you are quite able to step back out of? You will have become wet, and muddy, but you will dry out again, you can brush off the dirt, or have a change of clothes when next possible. None of this is a threat to you: it's not going to sink you. When you experience something another person says as feeling intensely bad for you, is it something you can reframe from posing a risk of drowning you to being something that is just a muddy puddle?

Improv to improve

One way of avoiding making a person feel criticised for something they've said is to always start your response with showing first that you're receiving what they've said and that you're receiving it in a way that is benign or positive rather than critical. In this way you're showing that you accept that this is their starting position (on the bridge) and they have their reasons for being in that position, so you can accept beginning with them from that position and go forward from there. In the field of improvisation in comedy, this principle is emphasised as the very basis from which any interaction can succeed. In comedy improv the rule is that whatever the other person offers you, you must always say, 'Yes, and . . .' Because if you say, 'No', the conversation stops.

Here is an example. I have been in social situations where a well-meaning person is trying to be friendly to me. They try to offer a conversational topic they think might be relevant to me, and because I am South African, they say, 'Have you been following the cricket/rugby [in which a South African team is playing]?' I would often answer by saying, 'No, that's not something I'm interested in'. End of conversation. I was being truthful, authentic, but I was not being skilful.

Using the 'Yes, and . . .' principle, when someone says this to me now, I will say something like, 'Yes I can see why you might imagine I'd be watching that. And you know, I never know whether I should support the team from the country I grew up in, or the country I live in now. What do you think?' In that way I am receiving what the person has said with acceptance, and finding a way to build on it, rather than rejecting their attempt at being friendly or making them feel they've said something inappropriate. And I'm staying with their topic, but subtly shifting it to a different focus: they are talking about a specific sports match, and I'm going from there to inviting a conversation about where your loyalties lie once you've immigrated, the latter being something I am more interested in and can more easily discuss than what's happened in a sports match that I've not watched. You can even use the 'Yes, and . . .' rule as a fun challenge for yourself – how can you take *any* conversational topic a person brings to you, and accept it ('Yes . . .') then build on it ('And . . .') with something related but which you are better able to contribute to?

Using the 'Yes, and . . .' principle is very helpful for how to manage a conversation, particularly with strangers and in general social situations where there is no task or agenda that sets the focus. How to begin or endure a conversation in such a context brings us to the topic of small talk.

Small talk

People are often disparaging about small talk, especially very high-IQ people. I think the first hurdle here is how you feel about yourself and about what your position is in relation to the people you're going to meet. It can be hard for a person with extreme intelligence to know what their position is. They're susceptible to feeling superior because their knowledge or complexity might be more advanced than that of others, but they're also susceptible to feeling inferior because their way of being has often not been understood or has been rejected. Also, they might be in a socialising situation which they would never have chosen for themselves but which has been imposed on them, like an obligatory workplace event, with people they don't expect they will enjoy mixing with. A first principle for successfully engaging in small talk is to transcend these old habits and fears and prejudices and deliberately approach any other person – in any situation – from the stance of 'I'm OK, you're OK'.

The term 'small talk' – putting the word small in front of the word talk – makes it sound like it is unimportant or of little consequence, that it is silly, or trivial. I have wondered: What does the word 'small' in 'small talk' actually mean?

I think small talk should be re-named as 'small risk talk'. And in that sense it is very important because it is the kind of talk that is designed to make the people who are starting to talk to each other feel comfortable with each other. It is a way to soothe. It demonstrates to the other person that you are not a threat to them, that it's safe to converse with each other. This is the necessary starting point for anything more to happen, because if someone is not feeling comfortable and safe, then they will not function well or open up or engage in things that are bigger or of more importance or higher risk.

In this sense, small risk talk is the essential starting point for conversation, to establish connection and create some sort of shared foundation, as a 'warm-up' to getting to know someone better or going deeper. You might think of small talk as being small in terms of importance of *content*, but it is big in terms of importance of *function*. Engaging in small talk involves the principle of 'playing along', introduced in Chapter 3. You know it is not profound in content, but you can understand and accept that it is necessary and therefore choose to play along with it. And if you accept this, then there is the possibility of elevating this to a level where engaging in small (risk) talk can also involve 'playing for enjoyment'. Here is an example of someone doing small talk superbly.

Small talk: the defecating dachshund

A friend of mine and I leave his house where he has recently moved to, and ahead of us we see two of his new neighbours, who are taking their dachshund for a walk. The dachshund stops to do its toileting and the neighbours stand waiting. Because they've stopped, we draw nearer to them, and as we're about to pass them, my friend stops beside them, but at a respectful distance, puts his hands behind his back, leans towards them with a huge smile, and, looking at their dog, says, 'Your dog has the optimal length of leg for the most agreeable dog-walking experience'.

The neighbours are a bit taken aback to suddenly have this charming man paying generous attention to something they have a special interest in – that is, their dog. My friend's whole body language shows that he is non-threatening – hands clasped behind his back, huge smile. The way he is leaning forward demonstrates his attentiveness towards them, his interest in them. His friendly smile sends out beams of warmth for them to bask in. They immediately laugh and smile back.

Then, taking his cue from their positive reaction, my friend continues:

> The legs are not too long, so you don't have to run to keep up with the dog or feel at the end of the walk that you haven't satisfied the dog because you've walked too slowly or not far enough for it. You can take the walk at your own leisure, knowing that this is still giving the dog really good exercise. And by the end of it you are both feeling satisfied. So, the optimal length of leg!

The neighbours laugh again, reciprocating with further beaming smiles of their own, and within seconds, they are treating my friend like he is their own best friend.

Let's look at why this was so effective.

First, my friend's timing of talking to his new neighbours was great, because he could see they already had a reason to temporarily stop.

Second, his body language gave all the cues of safety that would be uncon-sciously picked up by their autonomic nervous systems and put them in a state of safety, which is the state that is needed for the Social Engagement System (see Chapter 1) to function well.

Third, his choice of content was excellent for grabbing their attention in a positive way. It was an unexpected way of opening a conversation – 'Your dog has the optimal length of leg . . .' – but in a good way, because it is amusingly unusual, and relates to something they care about (their dog), and is positive (complimenting their choice of dog). So in other words, it creates a safe surprise.

The way my friend stopped gave the impression that he had all the time in the world for them, time to actually stop and really look at them, and notice something about their situation. This would boost their sense of worth, mak-ing them feel that they matter enough for him to give them his attention. He also immediately demonstrated empathy, that he was thinking about them from their perspective – everything he said was about imagining what walking their dog was like for them.

Also, he chose the positive angle on the topic. A dachshund's legs are an obviously noticeable thing about it because they're so short. He commented on this obvious thing, but from a positive angle that showed he appreciated its advantages. This validates the situation his neighbours are in, showing he is 'on their side', which puts them at their ease.

The opposite of this would be saying something negative like how ridiculous the shortness of their dog's legs is, such as 'Don't dachshunds look funny the way they waddle and try to keep up with you!' (which is criticism parading as humour) or 'Those short legs must really slow you down when you're trying to walk the dog' (which would be criticism parading as empathy).

My friend's whole exchange with his new neighbours lasted not more than probably five minutes before we were on our way again. It didn't take long, yet was a valuable investment in building good relationships for the future. This friend of mine is one of the most extremely intelligent people I know, who can talk with encyclopedic erudition on almost any topic, yet he had the generosity to initiate engaging in this little bit of small risk talk with people who are not (yet?) of any importance in his life. It was clearly fun for him too, leaving all concerned with a burst of feel-good hormones.

We can abstract from this story the steps to good small risk talk:

1   *Start with the mindset of 'I'm OK, you're OK'.* Avoid being apologetic, making covert digs, being critical of self or others, challenging someone or showing off – just be open-heartedly friendly and benign.
2   *Approach with non-threatening body language.* In other words, Soothe.
3   *Begin with a statement that is positive.* Bridge: accept whatever their starting point is, and offer empathy, showing you can think about what is going on for them from their perspective. And validate a person, pointing to what is already good about them and their situation, rather than pointing to how their situation is lacking or could be improved. Don't be dishonest – only say something you authentically mean.
4   *Check what their reaction is.* Based on how they react, develop your statement further, or try a different one. In other words, Titrate.

People hear things in different layers. There is the conscious layer of the meanings of the words said. There is the less conscious layer of the accompanying body language. And there is the unconscious subtext or more subliminal interpretation of the interaction. When my friend spoke with his neighbours about the optimal dog-walking experience, a deeper layer or theme was that he was describing an experience of things going well between beings, finding a compatible pacing between you that leads to mutual satisfaction. This sends a great subliminal message to new neighbours about how things could go well between you.

And my friend's description of how the pacing of a dog walk creates satisfaction is exactly applicable also to how the pacing of a conversation creates satisfaction.

Small talk and free association

A capacity for 'free association', a term coined by Freud,[7] is a great aid to small (risk) talk, and to general conversation. Free association is when you non-judgementally report whatever comes into your mind. You can start anywhere at all, knowing that reporting whatever comes to mind in a non-judgemental way will lead somewhere interesting.

Free association is similar to stimulating conversation. Stimulating conversation involves freely moving from topic to topic and sharing what comes to mind on that topic, without fear or judgement. This is also what creativity entails: creativity is about looseness of associations and a willingness to try things out without being worried about where it will go. Creativity requires a willingness to make mistakes, and you can only be creative in conversation if you feel the freedom that if you do make a mistake, you will still be accepted, or if you feel confident that even if your mistake causes upset, you know how to work to repair it.

People who have had negative social experiences, and feel they are outsiders/misfits and are likely to be rejected, will have much higher self-censorship and will be afraid to be creative in conversation. In conversation they will be 'playing for safety' rather than 'playing for enjoyment'. Building your skills for soothing others and for soothing yourself are ways of promoting more freedom and enjoyment in conversation.

Let's give this a try.

For an example of free association, I will free associate to the topic of . . . mountains. I'm going to tell you, the reader, whatever comes to my mind about mountains.

What do you think of mountains? I see mountains as enduring, a bit out of reach, beautiful, potentially dangerous. When I say 'mountains', what season do you picture – spring? Snowy winter slopes? (What is your favourite season?) If you had to choose, would you rather live in the mountains or by the seaside? Do you like to climb mountains? Some people find climbing mountains too slow or tedious. Maybe instead of climbing up mountains, you would prefer to ski down them? Exhilarating. The beautiful scenery and views at the top. Do you find being close to a mountain impressive, consoling, or does it make you feel oppressed, being towered over? The shadow it casts over the house if you live at the foot of a mountain, the way it restricts your view of the horizon. When I lived near Table Mountain, I would drive every morning from my side of the mountain (Tamboerskloof) to the University of Cape Town over on the other side, and sometimes there would be different weather conditions on the different sides of the mountain, and I would have to re-tune my radio because the signal was slightly different on the other side. Other mountains of the world — Mt Kilimanjaro, the Rockies, Everest. Stories involving mountains, a favourite childhood story of mine is Heidi, *which is set in the Swiss Alps (I could tell you the things I loved about that story). Another story set in the mountains, a film, is* The Sound of Music — *people tend to love it or hate it, what do you think of it? Have you seen that film* 127 Hours, *where the man gets stuck while mountain-climbing and gets trapped, and he cuts off his arm because that is the only way he can free himself and survive? My colleague who died in a mountain-climbing accident . . .*

Free associating like this reminds me of the game where you time each other to speak for one minute on whichever topic the other person chooses. You have to speak with no hesitation, repetition, or deviation; otherwise, you are out. This is great practice for being presented with a topic and seeing what you can find to say about it.

You can see from my sample free association on mountains how many different things that starting point can lead to — preferences about places to live, experiences of or knowledge about other countries, childhood memories, favourite books, films, daily routines you've experienced.

I enjoy noticing in films and novels how characters first meet. What brings them together? How does their conversation begin? What do they cover in what they say to each other?

When you get good at small risk talk and freer in your conversation, and the conversation between you and others becomes more enjoyable, you will have opportunities to move that interaction into something more regular. By becoming friends.

How to make a friend

Some friends are instant. You meet in a context that brings you together like school or university or work and make a connection that lasts a lifetime. Even if you don't see each other for a few years, when you get together again, it feels like you've never been apart. Other friends come after a long time of having some sort of acquaintance with each other. Something changes, and you move it to a different level.

This is represented in Figure 6.1, which conceptualises how social relations develop and change over time.[8] It shows three concentric circles around you. The people most involved in your life occupy one of these circles: close to you, closer, or closest. Throughout your life people can move in and out of these circles, or move back and forth between the circles.

For example, if you become friendly with someone at work, but you only see them there, then your involvement with each other is dependent on working together, so it is fully role dependent. If either of you leaves that job, and you don't see each other again, they move out of the circles altogether. But if you start making efforts to spend time together outside of that job, they will

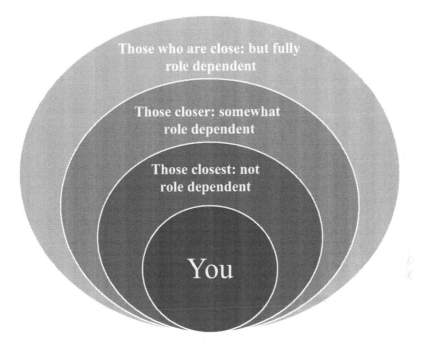

Figure 6.1 People in your life: how social relations develop and change over time

move closer to you, from the outer circle to the middle one. When seeing each other is no longer exclusively within the context in which you first met, the friendship is no longer fully role dependant.

But perhaps when you see each other, you still only really talk about work. They are closer to you, but still somewhat role dependent, because if either of you were to completely leave the occupation or interest you originally shared, you might lose touch as you no longer have enough in common that motivates spending time together.

The people closest to you are not role dependant. It doesn't matter what they, or you, are doing in life, what your interests are, or where geographically you live, the relationship is closest because you talk with each other about any or all things of significance in your lives and know that you are always there for each other emotionally (and also practically when logistics permit).

All through your life, people can move in and out of these different circles. For example, your intimate partner would be in the closest circle, a relationship that is not role dependent. If you separate and remain in regular contact but only to negotiate issues related to your children, that person has moved to the fully role-dependant layer – without their role as co-parent of your children, you would no longer stay in contact with that person.

But how can a friendship begin, or move between layers? As with all relationships, this relies on Soothing, Bridging, and Titrating. When you make a good connection with someone, it is because you both experience a state of safety with each other. With them you experience that you can express yourself with freedom and are accepted. (So interacting with them brings you into the 'Thriving' quadrant.) You have a good bridge intact between you, and the way you relate to each other is reciprocal (titration is operating well between you).

Let's concentrate on your part in this. It begins with you sharing of yourself (giving away information for free) and showing acceptance of what the other person shares of themselves. Show that you're noticing things about them, paying attention to who they are, but focusing on things about themselves that they're likely to appreciate you noticing as opposed to things they are uncomfortable with that will 'hit a tender horn'.

Offer to do things for them. Invite them to things. But incrementally. Always titrating, noticing their reaction, and keeping things even, so that you're not doing too much from your side without reciprocation from them.

Give them positive feedback. Let the person know what you enjoy about them, that you're thinking of them, and looking forward to seeing them. Show them that you remember things they've told you and things you've done together – refer back to such things. In this way you show them they are becoming important to you.

Strengthen the bridge between you. Name the similarities between you, the areas of overlap in your interests that you appreciate, and also positive ways in which your differences benefit each other. For example, 'You're so good with direction, which I'm hopeless at, but I'm great at planning good itineraries, which you have no patience for. So together we make perfectly compatible travel companions!'

Again, always Titrate, keeping it even, not forcing or demanding from the other person, so that moving closer is a mutually voluntary development. Never expect everything from one person – be grateful for whatever works well with a person, notice what that is, and value and nurture that. Avoid unintentionally pressuring them into being something different than they are.

Keep seeing people, even those closest to you, as Shakespeare's snail. Keep Soothing to reinforce your respect for them and acceptance of them Keep Bridging to understand better who they are and how they experience things, and to share with them who you are and how you experience things. Keep Titrating, noticing their reactions and adjusting your communication accordingly. Relationships that have seemed solid for years can begin to fall apart if either of you stop experiencing being in a state of safety with the other.

Over a lifetime people move closer together or apart for all sorts of reasons – as the saying goes, 'a lot of water passes under the bridge'. If something seems to be going wrong in a relationship, you can do your best to repair it, but it has to be mutual: if the other person does not reciprocate, you may have to accept letting them go. But still do this with courtesy towards them – you never know whether you might come together again at a different stage in your lives and how you might relate to each other then. In other words, don't burn bridges.

When letting go is necessary, know that you can survive without any one specific individual. You might prefer to have them in your life because you enjoy – even love – them, and they enhance your life, but if you were to lose them, you would survive. Loved ones might leave the country. They might die. Even if you feel utterly bereft, with time and care you can adjust to loss.

Each person is unique and the way you relate to each person will be unique. If you lose them, you will be upset, mourn them, miss them, miss the part of you they brought out in you, and always remember them and be grateful for what you had together. But your survival does not depend on any one person's continued regular involvement in your life. As long as you keep using your seven essential IT'S BETTER communication skills with people you encounter, you can keep making new unique connections, making other good relationships that you can value and contribute to and be nourished by.

If you would like to reflect on this, I suggest drawing the circles from Figure 6.1 and writing down the names of people in your life past and present, placing their names in the circles in which you feel they belong. Can you see how people close to you have moved between circles? Is there a balance of people occupying the different circles in your life, or would you like to have more people within a particular circle? Is there someone you would like to be closer to, or less close to, whose position in the circles you would like to actively work to shift? How might you do that?

Do try this at home – Chapter 6 boxout

I would like to invite you to reflect on this question: *What makes a conversation great?*

In a job interview I attended for a lecturing post, I was asked this: 'Describe a teaching session that you thought went very well, and describe what made it go well'. I think that's a wonderful question, which can be applied to teaching sessions but also to conversations.

Here are two more true-life situations, both related to therapy.

Situation no. 1: A therapist described how at the end of her work with a client, the client was full of praise for how that had been their best ever experience of therapy, and how wise and helpful the therapist had always been. The therapist was stunned to hear this because her perspective was that through all the sessions with this client, she had hardly said anything.

Situation no. 2: A client had a first session with a prospective therapist. The client described that in that first session the therapist demonstrated impressive knowledge and incisive brilliance, saying things about the client that showed the therapist had deep insight into how the client functioned as a person. The client never went back to that therapist again and searched for a different therapist to work with instead.

What do you think was going on in these two situations? Can you explain with reference to any of the IT'S BETTER seven essential communication skills?

How to appreciate good conversation

Here is an activity for you to try out:

1   Describe a conversation that you thought went very well.
2   What is the main thing about it that stood out for you?
3   Describe how it affected you: how did you feel during the conversation, and how did it leave you feeling afterwards?
4   Describe what you think made it go well.
5   Now, look back over your description. How many of the IT'S BETTER seven essential skills can you see in operation within your example of a great conversation?
6   Contact the person you had this conversation with and give them positive feedback. Tell them how much you appreciated it. Say something specific about what you liked about it and how it affected you. And thank them for it!

Notes

1   Kundera (1982, pp. 79–80).
2   For anonymity this is not her real name.
3   Winnicott (1969, p. 711).
4   For example, see Ackerman and Hilsenroth (2003).
5   Rogers (1959, 1961).
6   Not their real names.
7   See Freud (1917/1991, p. 328).
8   This is based on the Convoy Model of social relations. See Antonucci et al. (2014).

References

Ackerman, S.J. and Hilsenroth, M.J. (2003). A Review of Therapist Characteristics and Techniques Positively Impacting the Therapeutic Alliance. *Clinical Psychology Review*, 23, pp. 1–33.

Antonucci, T.C., Ajrouch, K.J. and Birditt, K.S. (2014). The Convoy Model: Explaining Social Relations from a Multidisciplinary Perspective. *Gerontologist*, 54(1), pp. 82–92. doi:10.1093/geront/gnt118.

Freud, S. (1917/1991). *Introductory Lectures on Psychoanalysis*. Translated by J. Strachey. London: Penguin.

Kundera, M. (1982). *The Book of Laughter and Forgetting*. London: Faber and Faber.

Rogers, C. (1959). A Theory of Therapy, Personality and Interpersonal Relationships as Developed in the Client-Centered Framework. In S. Koch (ed.) *Psychology: A Study of a Science. Vol. 3: Formulations of the Person and the Social Context*. New York: McGraw Hill.

Rogers, C. (1961). *On Becoming a Person: A Therapist's View of Psychotherapy*. London: Constable.

Winnicott, D.W. (1969). The Use of an Object. *The International Journal of Psychoanalysis*, 50, pp. 711–716.

7 Difficult conversations (including conflict resolution)

What makes a conversation difficult? You may feel a need to ask or tell someone something, or initiate a change, but you don't know how. Or perhaps there is already an awkward situation or history between you. This can make you dread future interaction because you fear it could once again be an unpleasant experience or make things worse. Or you could be in, or on the brink of, a full-blown conflict with someone. Any of these situations can feel harder within relationships that have become entrenched in habitual patterns (such as within families or between couples) and/or there is a power dynamic involved (such as employer/employee).

A difficult conversation is when the bridge between you starts feeling more like a tightrope, about to snap.

Finding it difficult to talk with someone is mostly about being concerned about how they will react. If you knew that anything at all you said would be received in calm acceptance, no big emotional reaction, no criticism, and they would never use it against you, then you might imagine you'd have no problem with saying anything at all. Yet these conditions are exactly what a psychotherapist provides, and in therapy sessions people still have things they find hard to talk about. Even when they know these conditions are in place, a lifetime of conditioning makes them cautious about what they say.

You cannot control how another person will react, but you can develop skills that will give you courage to manage your end of a difficult conversation well, maximising the likelihood of a good outcome and minimising the chances of causing damage.

The lost connection

A conversation becomes difficult when you feel you are starting to lose connection with the other person. I'm sure we've all experienced being on a mobile phone conversation when the other person's voice starts breaking up. It's frustrating, you don't know whether you're being heard, you can no longer properly follow what the other person is saying. These are exactly the same

DOI:10.4324/9781003029106-11

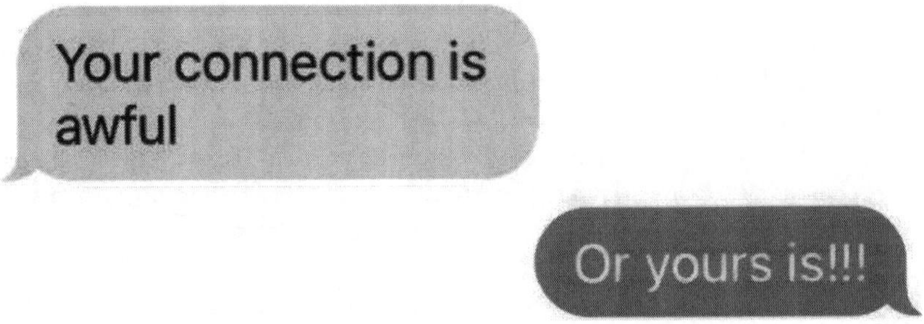

Figure 7.1 The lost connection

feelings that come up even in a non-digitally mediated, face-to-face conversation, when you don't like something that's been said. You begin to lose connection with the other person.

And as soon as the connection starts breaking up, what almost always happens is what's depicted in Figure 7.1. It is an image of a screenshot of a text one of my sons sent me, and my reply, when a mobile phone conversation between us started breaking up.

This phone screenshot in Figure 7.1 depicts how when a connection begins to be lost, each person almost instantly assumes the fault must lie with the other person. This is called projection: you keep yourself feeling good and safe and blameless by projecting anything problematic onto the other person.

A starting point in how to manage difficult conversations, is to recognise that this is what happens, and to hold off from engaging in knee-jerk projection. Because the reason for the lost connection might be on your side, and reconnection will be jeopardised if you're not able to acknowledge and address this. I will explain three important principles related to navigating difficult conversations, then discuss examples in the contexts of friendship and family dynamics.

Important principle no. 1: Reinforce 'best self', or Wise mind

It's important to recognise that every person is made up of their 'best self' plus 'messier' parts of themselves they are less comfortable with and would prefer to keep concealed. All major psychological approaches have terminology that acknowledges this insight. Freud called the messier parts of ourselves that we try to keep under control the 'id'.[1] Carl Jung called it our 'shadow'.[2] Professor Steve Peters called it our inner or hidden 'chimp'.[3] We strive to operate from our best self and hope that is the part others will see. We might split our and others' best self into 'good', and the messier parts into 'bad'. (This is a relic from childhood, where we may have been called a 'good child' or 'bad child' according to our behaviour.)

When we become dysregulated (upset, tired, hungry, afraid, angry), it's harder to present our best self, and we may say things or behave in ways we later regret. Conversations become instantly more difficult when someone is dysregulated. Dysregulation presents the risk that either or both people will make that split into 'good' versus 'bad' and start seeing the other person as bad.

Remember from Chapter 1 how we are always scanning for safety versus danger, at the unconscious level of neuroception. In our autonomic nervous system's alertness to danger, 'bad' means 'threat'. The neuroception of danger triggers in us a state of defence, ready to fight or flee or freeze for our own protection. And when we are in a state of defence rather than a state of safety, the Social Engagement System is not in operation. Losing sight of the good in the other person, or even in yourself, is when behaviour can become more reckless and cause damage that can be harder to come back from and repair, to retrieve what is valued between you and the other person.

Another way of thinking about our 'best self', is that this is when our Wise mind[4] is operating (see Chapter 1). When Wise mind is functioning, we are not solely in the throes of an emotional reaction, nor solely trying to be reasonable and rational, but we are integrating both Emotion mind and Reason mind to deal with a situation more holistically.

Important principle no. 2: Distinguish between intention and impact

Generally, no one wants any conversation to go wrong. What you say to someone might have an unintended negative impact you didn't foresee. And it is the same for the other person – recognise that if you're becoming dysregulated by something they've said, perhaps that is not what they intended.

In such situations, it is helpful to make a statement that separates intention from impact. For example, 'I can see I've upset you with what I've just said. It was not my intention to upset you'. Or, 'I feel really angry about what you've just said. I'm sure it wasn't your intention to anger me'.

In this way, you show the other person that even though something difficult has happened between you, and a reaction has been triggered, you are reminding them of your best self (you didn't want to upset them), and you are remembering their best self (you believe they didn't want to upset you).

The more you can keep the 'best selves', or Wise minds, doing the talking during the difficult conversation, the more chance you have of maximising a good outcome and minimising damage.

Important principle no. 3: Use the IT'S BETTER essential communication skills

In approaching a difficult conversation, all seven of the IT'S BETTER skills are helpful, with an emphasis on the top three: Soothe, Bridge, Titrate. When you make a statement that separates intention from impact, it acts as a Soothe skill. The 'best self' is the one that feels safest, so referencing the best selves of both of you gives a soothing message of safety.

Referring to the concept of intention acts as a Bridge skill, because it recognises that what was in your mind, or in the other person's mind, might not have been effectively communicated and would be helpful to understand. It opens the possibility of showing curiosity about what that intention was and how this can best be conveyed.

By naming intention versus impact you are making a statement about the process of the conversation, which takes a temporary step away from the content of whatever you were talking about. This creates a pause, slowing down the conversation. This allows you to strengthen the Titrate skill by creating the opportunity to find out droplet by droplet what it was in the content of what was said that caused which reaction. If there is a difficult reaction, either of you can play 'pause and rewind', where you ask to pause the conversation and go back to find out what happened. In this way, you create the chance to deal with things incrementally rather than continuing with an uncontrolled rapid torrent of content that overwhelms.

A conversation you are having with someone might suddenly become difficult when you didn't expect this, or you might have an upcoming conversation that you already anticipate will be difficult. Either way, the IT'S BETTER skills will equip you to manage difficult conversations.

How to approach what you anticipate might be a difficult conversation

I have found in my psychotherapy practice that many clients forego saying the things they want or need to say because of not knowing how practically to begin, what actual words to use, what steps to take, and how to manage whatever might arise for themselves or the other person during the conversation. Having extreme intelligence does not make this easier. As soon as Emotion mind[5] gets triggered, Reason mind, no matter how clever it is, can become disengaged, posing the risk of the person becoming dysregulated and an unwelcome outcome of fight or flight or freeze.

When a client tells me about a potentially difficult conversation, we can think this through together in advance, by engaging in the Reflect skill. As well as the Reflect skill being step 7 of a communication cycle (see Chapter 4, Figure 4.1), when used to reflect on a conversation after it has ended, the Reflect skill can also be step zero of any conversation, to reflect in advance on what might be involved to help prepare for the conversation. Here is an example of how I worked with a client to help him prepare for an impending difficult conversation.

Client example: a difficult conversation with friends

James[6] was a university student who experienced a breakdown and had to take time out from his studies (termed 'rustication'). He was very upset about how this meant he had missed out on important relationship-building experiences with the university friends he'd made prior to rusticating. He had started seeing these friends again but said it felt superficial, and he didn't know how to move his interactions with them to a level that felt more meaningful.

A first hurdle was that he didn't know what to say about his rustication. The fact he had been absent for a period was like the elephant in the room that he didn't know whether to mention, or how. Might others want to avoid it because they were uncomfortable with it or because they feared it would make him uncomfortable?

When reflecting in advance on a potential conversation, it is necessary to always start by ascertaining what your own intention is for that conversation. What outcome do you want? James wanted the outcome of less superficiality in his friendships. But in terms of 'the elephant in the room' (his rustication), how did he feel about the situation? Did he want to talk about it, or avoid it?

We discussed what things had been like for him with these friends the last time he saw them, how he felt about that, and what he hoped for the next time. He said he longed to talk about his feelings but this was unfamiliar and felt awkward and difficult for him. Having ascertained that his intention was to talk about his rustication rather than avoid it, we could prepare for how he might go about this. He could even rehearse it with me in advance.

I explained the Soothe skill and suggested that he thinks of a few appropriate Soothe topics that he could go into the conversation prepared with. These could act as a backup plan to draw on in any awkward moment or provide an exit route when he wanted to move away from a topic. What topic was mutually easy for him and his friends to talk about? He said they had all been involved in rowing together, and there was a rowing competition coming up, so he could easily talk with them about rowing.

We agreed that when he next saw his friends, he would have in mind his intention to have a more meaningful conversation with them about his rustication, and he would arrive prepared with the Soothe topic of rowing as a backup plan and be on the lookout for what might be a good moment for broaching the subject of his rustication.

Finding the right time to mention something is part of the Tune skill. I talked with James about how tuning means first checking what state he is in and what state the friend is in. Is this a good time to talk, in terms of being able to give each other lucid attention? (Not being drunk or constantly interrupted, and being able to hear each other properly. Checking that the other person seems receptive to conversation – that their attention is on him, rather than being distracted or in a hurry to do something else.) Taking a few breaths to help put himself in a state of safety.

The next step would be to start the conversation with the Soothe skill of saying something that helps relax the other person and puts them in a state of safety. (Something as simple as, 'It's great seeing you again. I've been hoping for us to have a chance to talk more'.)

Next, would be the Bridge skill. Naming the desired subject. In this way James would take a step towards the other person on the bridge by making it clearer to them what's going on for him, giving away information for free. For example, 'I feel like there's this elephant in the room: I've had this time away and we haven't mentioned it between us. Maybe both of us don't know how to broach it!' (Making a 'both of us' comment gives a message of 'We're in this together', which is soothing, suggesting yourselves as being together rather than apart.)

He could give away more information for free. ('I want you to know I'm comfortable with talking about my rustication', or 'I'll admit it's not exactly easy for me to talk about my rustication, but I'd like to try because I don't want to ignore it'.) I highlighted that he doesn't have to wish or pretend he's not where he is: accept what his own starting point is on the bridge, and let the other person know more about what that is so he helps the other person reach him.

Then he could invite them to take a step towards him on the bridge, to make themselves clearer to him, by inviting them to tell him where they are with that subject. ('I wondered what you think about that?' or 'I don't know whether there's anything you'd like to say about that or ask me about it?')

The Expand skill, in this context, would be for James to think about things like, what does he know about this person's perception of or attitudes towards rustication? Being aware of the wider context can help him pitch the way he talks about it with this individual.

Employing the Titrate skill would mean James noticing the person's reaction to what he said. Do they look uncomfortable? (Breaking eye contact, looking away, physically turning or stepping further away from him, ignoring what he's said, changing the subject.) If they show discomfort, he can Soothe again. ('No problem – we don't have to talk about this. Just thought to bring it up in case it helps but no worries.') Then bring up the planned Soothe topic. For example, 'So, how's it been going with rowing – there's that competition next weekend, I imagine it's pretty full-on at the moment?' (This comment has offered empathy – which involves showing that you're imagining what is important to the other person and what they're experiencing, which is a Bridge skill.)

If a person shows discomfort with a subject you've raised, it might just mean they need more time to prepare for having that conversation, because they weren't expecting it. Sometimes a person shows discomfort, and you provide an exit route, and then on a subsequent occasion they come back to you with it, themselves raising the subject and showing that they are now ready to discuss it. Because you showed transparency and courtesy in the way you previously broached the subject, they will already be feeling more safe with you at the beginning of the next conversation.

I told James that if the person shows they are comfortable with the subject he's raised (they make eye contact, turn or step towards you, or engage directly with the topic), then great, he can proceed with the conversation. But I cautioned against launching into a whole speech about everything that led to the rustication, what it was like, the fact he's back now, and so on. He should use the Titrate skill. Say a bit, check their reaction, gauge whether they want more, and give and receive feedback.

Also, he could step back from the content of the conversation at any point and make a comment on the process. For example, he could say, 'Oh I'm so glad we're addressing this elephant' or 'It's a relief to finally talk about this with you' or 'Thanks for being so nice about this. You've made it easy for me to talk with you about this'. (These comments involve continuing to give away information for free, strengthening the bridge, plus they are soothing, because they're saying positive things to the other person – validating them and showing appreciation – which will make them feel increasingly safe with him.)

When he's had enough of discussing that subject, or can see they have, he can use the End skill. Make a statement to clearly signal an ending, such as, 'I'm really glad we've got to acknowledge this thing together, so hopefully we'll both feel more comfortable about it in future'. (Another 'we're in this together' message.) Then bring out the prepared Soothe topic. ('What I'm really wondering about now and would love to hear about, is how you're getting on with rowing?')

Afterwards, he would move on again, full circle, to the Reflect skill. Reflection can take place on your own, or with someone else. James would be able to reflect with me in his next session on how it went.

In this preparatory conversation with me, James said he found approaching the issue in this way very different. He said it was really interesting for him to see me experimenting with different phrases he might use, because he hadn't thought about it that way before, that you can think about and practice with what words you could say. (So here he was giving helpful feedback to me.)

People with extreme intelligence tend to think they should be beyond taking such simple steps, that they should have a good vocabulary and complex mental functioning that takes them straight to the right thing to say – in the same way they might be familiar with getting straight to the conclusion of a mathematical problem without being aware of what steps they took to get there, but they get the right answer. In interpersonal interaction, being humble and patient enough to slow it down, look at the steps involved, and think about the actual words being used – even simple words – can give a person the preparation they need for being able to approach the thing they've been dreading and avoiding.

In James's next session he reported having carried out the plan exactly as we'd discussed, and what a revelation it was to him. At the next social gathering he was at, he broached the subject of his rustication with a friend. She was clearly relieved that this significant issue was no longer being ignored. He gave her permission to mention it, and he led the way, showing her he was all right with 'going there'. During the conversation, she gave away information for free, explaining her personal experience with mental health issues. This added to the data bank he could draw on in future conversations with her, helping him know more about her that he could add to his awareness when employing the Expand skill during future conversations with her. The whole conversation went very well.

I have found when I do this with clients, preparing for a difficult conversation, suggesting and practising with words that can be used, they often say to me, 'When you say it, it sounds so simple and easy', and they often want to write down what I've said. This helps them try out possible phrases and personalise them to what would feel most natural for them to say.

This example with James has involved a friendship situation. I will look at family relationships next.

Family dynamics

In American television drama *The Affair*, there is an episode[7] in which a mother pulls her husband to listen with her outside the bathroom door. They can hear that inside the bathroom their teenage daughter Whitney is throwing up. The mother tells her husband she's worried Whitney has an eating disorder, but cautions him that they must not say anything to Whitney about this because it will only alienate her, so they must be really careful how they handle it with her (using Reason mind). Next thing the bathroom door opens, and the mother immediately directs a blast of interrogation at her daughter like a burst of gunfire, asking what's going on, does she have bulimia, should they send her to therapy? She has instantly gone directly against all her own best advice (Emotion mind took over). The daughter looks at her parents with resigned disgust and walks away saying something like sure, they should just go ahead and do whatever they think is best. (Turns out the reason she's getting sick is that she's pregnant.)

This demonstrates how hard it can be within relationships where there are entrenched patterns and histories to even follow our own best advice about how to communicate most effectively. Your relationship with your family began when you were young and vulnerable and completely dependent, and established its dynamics over a very long period of time. This means that family members create a view of you during early years that you probably won't even remember, and their view can be hard to shift. Often big changes to who you are occur after you move out from living full-time with your family. Because they're seeing less of you, they more easily stay fixed on their original view of you and can find this hard to update. That can have the disorienting effect of feeling yourself pulled back into that prior version of yourself when you interact with them, which can feel unwanted and hard to know how to manage. Even if you have moved to a different country from your parent/s or siblings, you probably find when you visit them or speak on the phone, that you get pulled back into the old dynamics in ways you might not know how to make sense of or exert any influence over.

These old dynamics might also include games or locked-in complementarities (see Chapter 3, 'Playing the game'). Becoming aware of this can help you be prepared, and you can develop skills for better choosing how you want to behave during family interactions rather than automatically going along with old dynamics when these are unwanted.

I will present here an example that not only contains that power of family dynamics but was even more difficult because the historic dynamics involved abuse. Abuse creates long-lasting trauma and leaves the person feeling even more afraid of what an interaction might be like.

Client example: a difficult conversation with a parent

When Luke[8] started therapy, he began talking for the first time in his life about his abusive father. He had managed to stay in contact with his father by largely putting out of his attention the difficult dynamics and traumatic history and just placating his father to make their interactions as smooth as possible. When he started talking about the violence in therapy it stirred up strong emotions that made him feel unable to continue in this placating way, and he broke contact with his father, feeling that he needed some time and distance away from him to address the past and process its impact on him.

Two and a half years after this, Luke arrived at a session and told me his father had made contact again by sending Luke an email in which he asked Luke to phone him. Luke had not yet made any reply. Luke told me he felt afraid, not knowing how to manage an interaction with his father – this dominating, violent person. He felt that if he spoke with his father he might well just revert to the placating person he used to be, trying to pretend everything's okay. But he said he also feels angry and vengeful, as though he wants to wield power over his father, swing the power balance so that he is the one in control.

The necessary starting point in my conversation with Luke was, as always, to ascertain his intention. He was helpfully aware of his susceptibility to being pulled into old patterns – or old games – with his father. Did he want to be a pleaser, who ignores the difficult things? Did he still have any reason to be afraid, like he was when he was a child? Did he want to become the bully, because it was satisfying to no longer be the victim? (This would be a locked-in complementarity, where one of them remains the bully and the other the victim, even if they switch roles.)

Luke said he didn't want to be the bully. He didn't want to be pulled into this dynamic: his intention was to step outside of this locked-in complementarity. He made it clear that his intention was to hold onto all the progress he had made in therapy and approach any future interaction with his father from this new grown version of himself.

So Luke and I engaged in the Reflect skill together. We talked through how, before starting any interaction with his father, he would first Tune – breathe, keep himself grounded (including literally placing his feet firmly on the ground), trying to stay in Wise mind.

Luke then said that maybe he would speak to his father with a test, to first try and ensure his father had learnt from what had happened previously, and that he had changed, before he had any conversation with him. I said I could see that wanting to start with a test expressed his fear – it was a way he thought he could ensure his safety. But was such a test realistic – would his father ever change? Starting with a test would be imposing something on the other person. But what is in that person's mind? Why had his father made contact at that moment, for the first time in such a long time? Wasn't Luke curious to find out?

This hadn't even occurred to Luke, because he was so dysregulated by receiving contact from his father (Emotion mind had taken over). He said yes of course, he really did wonder why his father had made contact at that point. This would be the Bridge skill: finding out where the other person is coming from.

So we talked through the cycle of communication – Tune, Soothe, Bridge, and then Titrate. Titration is particularly important in a conversation where you are at risk of becoming dysregulated. I emphasised to Luke that during an interaction with his father, it didn't have to be all or nothing – no contact at all, or an experience that overwhelms him. And he is no longer the child who is trapped, captive to his domineering father who has access to him whenever he wants, and where Luke must do as he is told, dependent on his father for survival. Now Luke is himself a grown man. He can exert the control of managing the conversation bit by bit. He doesn't have to sign up to anything in advance – like forgiveness. Or – retaliation. Or – placation. He can simply take it moment by moment, notice what he is feeling, decide how he wants to behave in that moment. He can manage the conversation droplet by droplet, noticing his father's reaction, and keeping within his own capacity to cope, within his 'window of tolerance' (see Siegel, 2020). And any time he feels he's had enough, he can use the End skill to end the conversation. He has that power.

Luke said this was a very different approach. He had thought it was all or nothing, but now he could see he had other options. He said he was leaving the session feeling empowered, knowing he could remember these skills and strategies we had discussed and that these would support him to sustain all the progress he had made and not be pulled back into old ways. He also had the option of not phoning his father. He could choose to restrict communication to email instead if he didn't yet feel ready for talking.

At our next session, Luke was jubilant. Following our discussion, he had come to a point where he felt able to attempt a conversation with his father. So, he did phone him. They spoke again for the first time in two and a half years. Luke reported that they stayed on the phone for more than two hours, he had been able to maintain his new way of being throughout, and it had gone very, very well.

Feedback revisited

One kind of difficult conversation is when you have to give someone feed-back on something you have found difficult with them or want to ask them to change. Giving such feedback, as mentioned in Chapter 5, risks causing dysregulation in the recipient. So, how can you give feedback in a way that minimises this risk?

The typical directive to give feedback in a sandwich is about trying to mini-mise this risk. Sandwich feedback involves starting with something positive, then introducing what needs addressing, then ending with something positive again. We can say this model recognises the recipient of the feedback as being Shakespeare's snail. The positives offered are designed to soothe.

I think the best way of giving feedback is to invite the other person to reflect on the target issue and then engage in what they say with active listening (see boxout 'How to listen' in Chapter 4), rather than beginning by telling them what your view of the target issue is. This is hard, because someone with extreme intelligence will have a strong view of what the problem is and will be impatient to just say it candidly and tell the other person what to do about it. Also, it is time consuming to have a conversation in which you properly invite someone else's thoughts and experiences on an issue. It is much faster to just say, 'You didn't do that well enough, next time do it like this'.

Although that is faster, it is ineffective. It is the kind of approach that fuels the research findings that feedback not only does not improve performance, but actively makes it worse.[9] If you use open questions to invite the other person to reflect on the target issue ('How do you think [whatever] is going?', 'What's your view on [whatever]?'), you might find that they already raise the aspects you wanted to address. They might well already be aware there is a problem. If your invitation to them to talk has helped put them in a state of safety with you and they get to be the one who raises it, they have the chance to take ownership of it, rather than feeling criticised or shamed by you raising it, and this avoids dysregulation.

Conflict

When conflict arises – regardless of whether it is in the context of friendships, couple relationships, families, or at the workplace – it always involves the same principles. Conflict is when one person or more becomes dysregulated (pushing them into fight or flight or freeze) because they feel their concerns are being disregarded or threatened. The easiest way to intensify conflict is to keep ignoring that person's concerns. The quickest way to de-escalate conflict is to convince that person that you are taking their concerns seriously.

How can you convince the other person that you're taking their concerns seriously? First, you must find out *what* their concerns are. You might assume you already know what their concerns are. For example, a colleague and I went into a meeting with a student that she had requested with us. We knew it would be difficult because she had recently been investigated for fitness to practice, and we knew she was aggrieved about this, so we had every reason to assume this was what she was concerned about. We started the meeting by giving her a chance to fully say what was on her mind. To our surprise we discovered we had been wrong – it turned out it was her academic performance she was most worried about and wanted to discuss.

Finding out, fully and accurately, what the other person's concerns are is a Bridge skill. When people can no longer find out from each other what each other's concerns are and respond to these, a third party can help. When a warring couple goes to couple's therapy for help, the therapist becomes the bridge, working to help each partner see the other more clearly and understand better where each other is coming from, what they are feeling and needing.

In the field of mediation and conflict resolution, the mediator becomes the bridge, acting to discover what the concerns are of each party within the conflict and fashioning a compromise that best addresses these for each party.[10] If mediation fails or is not attempted, and people are in such serious conflict that they proceed with litigation against each other, each party uses a lawyer to emphasise and fight for their own concerns. In such a situation there is no bridging anymore, which often escalates the conflict, leading to battles that are protracted, distressing, and costly.

How to de-escalate and resolve conflict

You've probably had the experience of phoning your bank, or telephone or internet provider, in a state of frustration about something that has gone wrong with their service to you. A person answers the phone and you can hear they're in a call centre, probably in a different country. This makes you immediately feel more frustrated. Why? Because they feel further away from you on the bridge. If they're not even in the same country as you, then you may feel unsure that they will understand or be able to help with your concern.

You explain to them the problem, probably in a heated tone of voice because you were already annoyed at the issue you're phoning about and now in addition you feel unsure of whether they can help you. They say, 'Don't get cross with me, I'm only doing my job and I don't have any control over what's happened.' (They have gone straight into a state of defence, justifying that they are not the one at fault.)

Now you're becoming livid. You try to emphasise even more, maybe in a raised voice by now, how important your concern is. The other person is now probably experiencing you as angry. This conversation is not at all going well.

Imagine, instead, that when the person answers the phone they say, 'Hello. I'm based at a call centre in India but I will be able to ensure the right person is contacted who can help you. What is your concern?'

This helps soothe you, because they have named where they are on the bridge and what this means for your concern, which builds your confidence that something constructive will come out of this call. You explain the problem, in less heated tones, but still you are upset about the problem and the hassle of having to deal with it. The person on the other end of the phone says, 'I can understand how frustrating this issue is for you. You just need this service to work, don't you? I'll try to resolve things for you as soon as possible because I'm sure you're very busy.' Now you are completely soothed, you feel heard, understood, confident that your concern is being addressed, and you are talking with them in quiet tones, with respect and gratitude for their help.

Thinking about the way the above example escalated versus de-escalated the difficulty of the conversation, here are the principles for how to de-escalate and resolve conflict by using the seven IT'S BETTER essential communication skills:

I – As usual, always begin with 'I' – 'I am taking responsibility for my part in this'. Within difficult conversations, it is particularly important to use 'I' statements rather than 'you' statements. This means not focusing on the other person's behaviour, but rather focusing on how you have been affected. So instead of saying 'You did that [terrible thing]', which makes the person feel accused, say 'I felt [describe how you were affected] when you did that [neutral thing]'.

T – *Tune* in to the other person to check what state they're in, and to ensure this is the best time for having this conversation.

S – *Soothe* yourself in a conflictual situation by breathing. Soothe yourself and the other person by maintaining the 'I'm OK, you're OK' stance. This avoids splitting ('I'm the good guy, you're the bad guy', or the reverse), which risks developing locked-in complementarities. Even if you don't like what someone's done, talk to them from the position that they are OK, rather than that they're not OK. Say things like, 'You probably didn't realise . . .', 'I'm sure you wouldn't have wanted to cause upset', 'I know we're both trying our best . . .'

B – *Bridge*. Find out fully what the other person's concerns are. Make statements that show you're trying to understand where they're coming from and validating the position they're in from their perspective. Give away information for free about what your concerns are, and about how you interpreted something that happened. Make it clear that something is your interpretation, rather than a 'reality'. For example, instead of saying, 'You rushed through dinner so fast, you never have time for me!', say,

'During dinner you seemed rushed, which I interpreted as meaning I'm not important enough for you to spend more time with me, and now I'm feeling dejected'. The other person might be genuinely surprised to discover how you interpreted something.

E – *Expand.* Expand your awareness of the current issue. If a person is feeling slighted by you when no slight was intended, think about what else might be going on for them that contributed to them feeling this way. For example, have they been the victim of racism? They might be generalising that wound to the current experience, thinking this is more of the same. What is the essence of how they are feeling? If they are feeling overlooked or rejected or alienated or misunderstood, these are commonalities between us, whatever our individual differences are, because all humans want to experience being accepted, feeling safe, belonging. Talking about those similarities helps us connect with each other rather than focusing on differences that make us feel separated.

TT – *Titrate.* Deal with the issue little by little, rather than overwhelming someone with an entire manifesto about where you're coming from or what you think they've done wrong. At any point of titrating, you can choose to withhold the next droplet, and stop, or give one more droplet, all the time watching what the reaction is, and using open questions to clarify.

E – *End* the conversation in a courteous way, regardless of how it went. If feelings are running high, and perhaps it feels like the other person is trying to break down the bridge you've been trying to build, you can suggest taking some time out of the conversation and coming back to it later after you've (both) had a chance to calm down.

R – *Reflect.* This is your chance to really get in touch with your feelings about what's happened, start making sense of it, and decide what you'd like to do next.

Conflict avoidance versus rupture and repair

Sometimes people are so afraid of conflict that they do all they can to avoid it. They think avoiding conflict is what will make the other person feel safe with them and build a good relationship. They might feel that never having disagreement or conflict is what makes someone feel loved. What this misses, is the paradox that in order to feel truly loved by someone, first you must experience their hatred.

This paradoxical insight originates from psychoanalyst D. W. Winnicott.[11] It means that if you never see signs of someone disagreeing or being upset then you cannot deeply trust them, because they won't feel real to you – it is unrealistic that someone could always be in agreement and never be upset by anything. If you never see how they behave when they're upset, you could fear the worst. You don't have the certainty that even if they become angry, they will still be safe to be around. If you never disagree with me, how do I know whether you will reject me the first time we disagree, or still be respectful towards me even when we disagree?

If, on the other hand, you get to learn what someone struggles with, you feel more sure of who that person is, and that feels safer. If they show that they really hate something you said or did, and you experience that even in their hatred they remain benign and cause you no harm, then you can truly feel loved by that person, because you know what their worst looks like and that even when they are at their worst, they will still care for you.

Related to this, is the concept of 'rupture and repair', which originates in the work of psychoanalyst John Bowlby.[12] When any two people fall out of sync in the way they're relating with each other, such as having a misunderstanding or disagreement or full-blown conflict, this counts as a rupture in the relationship. For the relationship to survive, a repair to the rupture is needed (see the box-out at the end of this chapter on 'How to repair'). Research in attachment has demonstrated that it is the experience of repeated rupture followed by repair which *creates* security in a relationship.[13] The more often you experience that whatever goes wrong between you and I, I never harm you, and even if I get upset and angry I will always come back to you and make an effort to repair things and try to work it out with you, the more you will trust me.

We can take reassurance from these insights that finding ways to successfully navigate – rather than avoid – difficult conversations is eminently worthwhile if we want to build secure and enduring relationships with others within any context in our lives.

Do try this at home – Chapter 7 boxout

When something becomes difficult with someone, it is as though part of the bridge between you weakens or breaks. Believing that this is temporary and taking action to repair the bridge demonstrates resilience.

How to repair

- **First, notice there has been a rupture.** Rather than just leaving it and hoping it will go away, say that you've noticed it. This gives the chance to resolve it rather than having it deteriorate further through neglect. To borrow a phrase that travellers on the London Underground will be very familiar with hearing repeatedly: 'See it, say it, sorted.'
- **Ask if you can pause, and rewind.** Step away from the content of the conversation and focus on the process. 'Can we go back to the moment it got difficult and find out what happened there for both of

---

us?' If it is not possible to talk about it immediately, ask whether you can come back to it later at a time that suits you both and discuss it then.

- **Be ready to apologise.** Even if you don't feel you did anything wrong, recognise the difference between intention and impact, and be ready to say, 'I'm sorry for . . . [the impact I have caused: name what it is to show you understand how they feel affected]; that was not my intention'.
- **When discussing the rupture, be specific and stay focused on the current difficulty.** Avoid bringing up past issues or jumping to generalisations.
- **Keep your comments 'on your side of the bridge'.** Try to articulate as best you can what's going on for you, using 'I' statements about what you're thinking and how you're feeling affected, rather than using 'you' statements about what the other person did and what you think was going on for them. Make yourself clearer to them, and invite them to make themselves clearer to you.
- **Keep your 'best selves' in focus.** Be willing to believe the best of the other person, and of yourself. Say things like 'We have both found this difficult', 'I know we both really care about this', and 'We're both doing our best'. This helps 'save face' and avoids splitting either of you into 'the good guy' versus 'the bad guy'.
- **Be willing to see the difficulty as a temporary disruption.** Show that you believe there will be more interaction with each other in the future, which can be better than whatever is difficult right now.
- **Preserve the relationship.** Because you believe this is a temporary disruption, exercise damage limitation (don't burn bridges). Perhaps keep in mind a line that you never cross – for example, avoiding swearing, insults, low blows, aggression.
- **Recognise the bruises and be careful around them.** Don't ignore the damage caused by the rupture. Find out how the person is hurting – ask how they are feeling, and ask what will help to make it better.
- **Perform a gesture of goodwill to help strengthen the repair.** This is the equivalent of helping to 'clean up the mess'. Send them flowers and/or a card, and offer to do something for them to demonstrate you want to make things better.
- **Be resilient: try again.** Get back onto the bridge. Know that you will survive, your own bruises will heal, and what you can learn from what happened will benefit your future interactions.
- **Practice patience.** It might take a while for you, or the other person, to feel safe with each other again. That's okay – respect what time each of you might need to heal. In the meantime, keep making your interactions benign and soothing to win back confidence.

Notes

1 See Freud (1917/1991, pp. 21–27).
2 See Jung (1995).
3 Peters (2012, 2018).
4 Linehan (2015).
5 Linehan (2015).
6 For anonymity this is not his real name.
7 Season 1, Episode 8.
8 For anonymity this is not his real name.
9 See Kluger and DeNisi (1996).
10 For example, see Strasser and Randolph (2004).
11 Winnicott (1949).
12 Bowlby (1958).
13 For example, see Morton (2016).

References

Bowlby, J. (1958). The Nature of the Child's Tie to His Mother. *International Journal of Psychoanalysis*, 39, pp. 350–371.

Freud, S. (1917/1991). *Introductory Lectures on Psychoanalysis*. Translated by J. Strachey. London: Penguin.

Jung, C.G. (1995). *Memories, Dreams, Reflections*. Translated by R. Wilson and C. Wilson. London: Fontana Press.

Kluger, A.N. and DeNisi, A. (1996). The Effects of Feedback Interventions on Performance: A Historical Review, a Meta-Analysis, and a Preliminary Feedback Intervention Theory. *Psychological Bulletin*, 119(2), pp. 254–284.

Linehan, M.M. (2015). *DBT Skills Training Manual* (2nd ed.). New York: The Guilford Press.

Morton, M. (2016). We Can Work It Out: The Importance of Rupture and Repair Processes in Infancy and Adult Life for Flourishing. *Health Care Analysis*, 34, pp. 119–132.

Peters, S. (2012). *The Chimp Paradox*. London: Vermilion.

Peters, S. (2018). *My Hidden Chimp*. London: Studio Press Books.

Siegel, D.J. (2020). *The Developing Mind* (3rd ed.). New York: The Guildford Press.

Strasser, F. and Randolph, P. (2004). *Mediation*. London: Continuum.

Winnicott, D.W. (1949). Hate in the Counter-Transference. *The International Journal of Psychoanalysis*, 30, pp. 69–74.

8 Intimate conversation (including dating and romance)

Bowerbirds are renowned for the exquisitely elaborate structures the males build to attract a mate. All birds, and all animals, have courtship rituals that require steps to be taken in a sequence without which they will not be successful at mating. This is true of humans also.

People with extreme intelligence might disregard this, thinking they can see through it, it makes no sense, if they want a partner they should be able to just straightforwardly secure a deal (a bit like fictional geneticist Don Tillman in *The Rosie Project*, who wants a female partner and devises a questionnaire to assess the suitability of women he meets). But, as Don Tillman found, it is not as straightforward as that. 'Courtship' is an old-fashioned word, but it is a reality even in modern life and – with reference to the attitude described in Chapter 3 of 'playing along' – it's a bit like having to accept this and learn how to play the game.

I am a great believer in the joys of love and romance and the benefits of sharing your life with a compatible long-term partner. Desire for this, and trouble with this, is what brings many of my clients to consult with me. Success is very rewarding for them, and for me. One example is a note of gratitude a client sent me together with a photograph of herself smiling radiantly alongside her wife in their beautiful Indian wedding sarees – that image spoke volumes about what she had been through in her therapy in relation to her culture, her sexuality, her family's reactions, and her journey to courageous self-acceptance and self-expression, which led to her finding an accepting life partner with whom she can thrive. Being authentic in who you are is a pre-requisite for creating any fulfilling personal relationship.

Whatever your gender or sexuality might be, establishing a romantic relationship goes through three phases – flirtation, consolidation, and maintenance.

Flirtation

The display the male bowerbird puts on is a way of indicating to prospective females his suitability as a mate and what quality they can expect from him. In contemporary human life individuals often create this sort of display by posting an online dating profile. Even in this very first step of inviting attention

DOI: 10.4324/9781003029106-12

to yourself, which initiates the opening of a flirtation phase, you will have the greatest chance of success if you are authentic about who you are.

I had an extremely intelligent client who felt that his intellectual interests did not match his idea of what 'sexy' was. He used descriptions in his online dating profile that portrayed himself as what he considered more 'normal', in the way he thought would be most attractive to girls, but the girls who were attracted to that description would never maintain interest in him beyond a few conversations or a date or two. Because they would discover, obviously, that he was not what they expected. A bowerbird female wants a bowerbird male, not a swan or a stork parading as a bowerbird and hoping to get away with it.

There's a funny scene in the French series *Dix Pour Cent* (the version with English subtitles is named *Call My Agent*) involving actress Monica Bellucci. In a previous episode[1] she explained she was seeking a relationship, and that her fame tended to scare men off. In a later episode,[2] a man comes up to her at a party, clearly interested in her, and asks what sort of man she finds attractive. She says that all she wants is a regular guy, as though this would have the greatest chance of avoiding intimidating him. He immediately gets up and says, 'Too bad for me, then', and walks away.

Another favourite scene of mine is from the film *Wolf* where Jack Nicholl's character says to Michelle Pfeiffer's character that she is so afraid men will only be interested in her for her physical beauty that she tests them by behaving so objectionably towards them that there is nothing to recommend her personality, meaning that the only men who will hang around are precisely those who are only interested in her for her looks.

All this is to say: be true to who you are, even in the first display. If a prospective love interest falls away because you have shown who you are and it's not what they want, this is best for both of you, because both of you have the opportunity then to find someone who is a better match. I have worked with clients who have found wonderfully unique partners because they started being true to themselves, and that is a delight to see. Being true to yourself does not mean doing whatever you want in ways that disregard who the other person is. Beyond that first display, the next crucial aspect of flirtation is to apply all the principles of effective communication we've been examining so far.

All seven of the essential IT'S BETTER communication skills are relevant, but in the context of flirtation, the one I'd like to emphasise is the Titrate skill. You've heard of 'coming on too strong'. Or someone not realising the other person was interested because they maintained such careful diffidence. By using titration, you show interest and give a bit of attention, check what the reaction is, if it is positive, give a little bit more, and continue that way, always keeping it reciprocal. Depending on the individuals involved, this sequence could play out over months or even (like in 19th-century novels) years, or it could race from first catching each other's eyes across a crowded nightclub to essentially moving in with each other that same night, inseparable ever after. It does happen.

The most important thing for success is that the pacing remains reciprocal between both partners. In terms of attachment styles (see Chapter 1), a person with an avoidant style tends not to do enough 'giving away information for free' about who they are and what they want, so that the other person might find them stand-offish. A person with an anxious style has a tendency to blurt out everything they can about themselves as soon as possible. They have the fear that they will not be accepted by the other, and so they try to fast-forward the agonising process of wondering – it's like they are trying to say, 'Here is all of me, show me right now whether you're going to reject any of it so I can leave before we even begin and spare myself the heartache'.

But there is no fast-forwarding in relationships. They have to take place in real time. There is no getting around having to wonder if the other person is as interested as you are, fear rejection, and feel the excruciating anticipation of whether you will meet again or how it will be when you do.

If you can take this slowly, notice what you are feeling, and let it be, you can even savour it – the pleasure of it and the pain of it. Flirtation is a phase that is full of anticipation, moments of uncertainty, and arouses strong feelings which you might wish to escape by shutting it all down and withdrawing because it's too scary, or trying to foreclose the uncertainty and get married already. Being able to stay with the uncertainty and allow things to unfold at a mutual pace – whether that leads to deeper involvement or to separation – is invaluable for building sound relationships.

Falling in love is one of life's most wonderful experiences: your senses become heightened, the world feels like a different place, and you feel exquisitely alive. To help keep a hold of yourself during the process, first of all, breathe (see the Chapter 1 boxout). Second, re-read 'How to not be afraid of feelings' (the Chapter 5 boxout). Then you can work to develop what Marsha Linehan calls 'detached engagement'.[3]

Flirtation and beyond: detached engagement

'Detached engagement' sounds paradoxical. It means engaging with someone else, being able to become intimately involved with them, but from a position where you remain aware of your own self as a separate entity who continues to be viable independently. This means having the conviction that whether that person is in your life or not, you will still survive and enjoy and create value in your life. (This stance matches the 'I'm OK, you're OK' stance and helps develop a healthy interdependence, rather than the problematic state that has been termed 'codependence',[4] which is a stance of 'I'm not OK without you, and you're not OK without me'.)

With one of my clients we somehow got talking about this by using the analogy of sailing. He described his tendency, when he met someone, to 'get onto her boat', so that he would feel fully dependent on her for staying 'above water', as though he no longer had individual viability to stay well and find direction without her. I worked with him towards shifting this way of becoming involved to one in which he would 'stay on his own boat', taking responsibility for continuing to sail his own boat. He could draw confidence from maintaining his own viability, even though he would sail alongside her, even very close together. This meant they both enhanced their lives by accompanying each other on their journey but did so by each exercising the free choice of wanting to sail together rather than one person giving up their own boat and fearing they would sink unless they could stay on the other person's boat. (During the course of our work together, this client started taking actual sailing lessons, which he thoroughly enjoyed. By the end of our work together he was in a relationship unlike any he had been in before. In the last session I had with him his new partner joined him in the session and I had the pleasure of meeting her, and the three of us discussed together how to support their relationship to flourish.)

With detached engagement you can engage fully with someone you might dearly love and wish to have as a part of your life, but you detach yourself from the belief or expectation that having a good life depends on any one person. Whether you are together with someone or apart, you continue to take responsibility for looking after yourself and deliberately investing in your own well-being. This means you focus on remaining anchored in who you are, what your life is about, your own values and interests and goals, and you carry on looking after yourself, staying fit and healthy, and you continue nurturing your relationships with other people in your life also. By keeping your 'own boat' in good shape, you also keep yourself maximally interesting to and attractive to others, regardless of your relationship status.

Consolidation

As you get to know someone better and have become a couple, you enter the consolidation phase. In this phase, the Bridge skill is the one I want to emphasise. A client said to me,

> I was working out in the gym this morning when my new girlfriend walked in, and she just walked straight past me and didn't even stop to say hello and be friendly. So now I don't know if she's just very stuck up, or I don't mean very much to her, or maybe she's angry with me. It felt like she sees herself as superior to me, that she didn't want to be associated with me, had no time for me.

I said,

> All of those are possibilities. But there could be other possibilities also. What if she hadn't expected to see you there, and didn't know how to react? What if she is not confident about her body and felt self-conscious in her clingy lycra? Maybe she feared that if she came and chatted with you and you got a good look at her up close you'd find her lacking, so instead she just rushed to go and get on with her workout?

His jaw dropped. He said to me, 'That's exactly how she feels about her body.' And yet he had not taken that into account in that moment: he had been so worried about how she might view him as inadequate for her that he had not considered how she might be fearing she could be inadequate for him. Using the Bridge skill helps you find out what is in the other person's mind that is affecting their behaviour and helps you share with them what is in your mind.

Consolidation of a relationship is the phase in which you pass through certain milestones together that represent a deepening of your relationship and a growing mutual commitment to being part of each other's lives. Such milestones include: the first time you spend a whole weekend together; the first time you go away on a trip together; being introduced to each other's friends; meeting each other's parents; moving in together; and then other acts of long-term commitment like perhaps joining your finances, sharing symbols of commitment (like rings) or public ceremonies of commitment (like marriage), and getting a pet together or having a child together or adopting a child together.

People long for these things. They long for them so much that unfortunately they can be susceptible to being deceived by a promise that a relationship will develop this way, hanging on and hoping for more even when more never does materialise. Giving someone promises of more that never materialise has been called 'bread-crumbing'. Be aware of the difference between someone offering you crumbs and being offered the whole loaf.

It is also possible to be deceived by the appearance that you already have the whole loaf with someone when the true substance of consolidation is absent. This is how the 'Tinder Swindler' (see documentary by that title on Netflix) so successfully defrauded several women. I was amazed that the women concerned could believe they had a serious relationship with someone on the basis of nothing except very little time spent together, promises of plans for deeper involvement (like moving in together), and text messages that simulated love ('I miss you', 'I'm thinking of you', heart emojis). Digital simulation of love is very different from the real thing.

An important part of the consolidation phase involves finding a mutually comfortable rhythm of time spent together versus time spent apart. No two human beings can be together every single moment of every day, doing everything together. They might try – artists Marina Abramović and Uwe Laysiepen, known as Ulay, did just that with some very striking results, but it did not at all end well. (This included a spectacular walk towards each other on the Great Wall of China which was meant to culminate in their wedding, culminating instead in their final goodbye.)

In the previous section I mentioned how people with avoidant versus anxious styles of attachment might approach flirtation. During that phase, and all later stages of a relationship, if two people who have these contrasting styles try to form a relationship with each other, they will encounter the greatest difficulty. Because a person with an avoidant style needs distance, space, time alone, whereas a person with an anxious style always seeks proximity, closeness, time together.

The worst of the avoidant style can appear as uninvolved, cold, uncaring, and the worst of the anxious style can appear as overinvolved, clingy, smothering. When an avoidant person seeks time apart, the anxious person feels rejected and seeks reassurance by becoming clingy. The more clingy the anxious person becomes, the more uncomfortable or even repelled the avoidant person feels and the more they withdraw. You can see how this can become a self-perpetuating cycle that brings suffering to both individuals and often jeopardises the relationship.

The best fit is when two people with a secure style of attachment make a relationship with each other. A secure style can also work with the other styles because their security can compensate for their partner's avoidance or anxiousness. These styles are not set in stone: for example, psychotherapy can help a person develop a more secure style. I have written about the concept of 'fake it 'til you make it' – learning to behave in more secure ways even if you're not (yet) feeling secure, and how this generates reinforcing interpersonal rewards that in themselves help build more security.[5] Behaving as though you are already secure essentially means practising 'detached engagement' as described earlier, while using the Titrate skill to ensure your developing intimacy continues to be reciprocal and using the Bridge skill to genuinely get to know who each other are.

Even if two people in a relationship do not have the contrast of avoidant versus anxious as their dominant relational styles, a version of these dynamics can emerge any time when two partners become out of sync with each other because one is wanting more closeness or distance than the other. Sometimes external circumstances impose this: for example, in a settled and usually harmonious relationship, one person takes on a work project that makes them much less available to their partner. The partner's own circumstances have not changed, so they miss the attention they used to enjoy from their partner. They might start to fear that their partner's distraction and absence means a loss of affection, and they might protest against this, seeking more time together, more closeness, wanting reassurance that the partner is still invested in the relationship. This puts pressure on their partner, who could feel that what is being demanded from them at work is not being understood and they are not being supported by their partner, and this in itself could make them lose affection for the person who is being so unempathic.

Consolidation and beyond: projection in couple relationships

Part of getting to know someone involves navigating similarities and differences between the two of you. Differences can attract by being exciting and stimulating but can also repel when they feel threateningly foreign. Similarities are usually what give a sense of comfort, safety, and belonging.

The search for the comfort of similarity in relationships can make partners assume they understand the other. In his novel *The Unbearable Lightness of Being*,

Milan Kundera wonderfully explores misunderstood words between the lovers Franz and Sabina, showing how they think they know what each other mean and that they have a shared understanding of words like 'woman', 'music', 'betrayal', 'strength', whereas actually their individual experiences of and associations connected with these words are quite different from each other's. By using the Bridge skill you avoid projecting your assumptions onto the other person and instead find out from them more about what really is in their minds.

An important part of the consolidation phase is developing an optimal mix of how you manage being a separate individual while also being in a unit with your partner.

Figure 8.1 is a picture I drew for my students to explain this, showing a typical sequence that can happen in relationships and how to remedy it.

The first panel, (a), shows how two people meet, each with their own separate speech bubble, expressing who they are and what they're interested in. When they are attracted to each other, they choose to get closer and more involved with each other. That can lead to what is depicted in the second panel.

In (b), you can see that one person's speech bubble has fully incorporated the other person. This means that the grey person begins to view the other as being part of themselves, and assuming that whatever was in their own speech

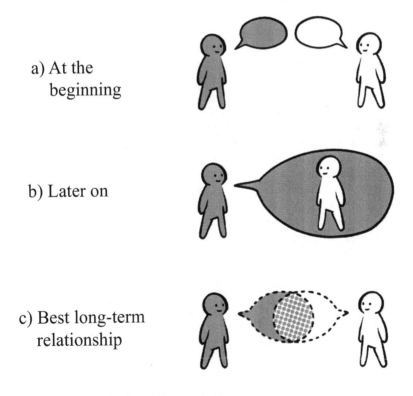

a) At the beginning

b) Later on

c) Best long-term relationship

Figure 8.1 How couple relationships can develop

bubble – their views, interests, and so on – will be similar for or pleasing to the other. It is like they have merged the other person with themselves. We can also say that the grey person is operating by projection: they are projecting all their own views and interests onto the other, creating a fantasy of who the other person is.

When this happens, if the person contained within the grey one's speech bubble is somewhat weak or passive or insecure, they might accept this, not behave in ways that challenge it, and might even be grateful for being incorporated in this way. They might be afraid that if they don't accept this projection – if they don't keep trying to be the fantasy the other is expecting of them – that they will lose that person's interest in them.

With one of my clients who had this pattern of relating to men, we referred to it with each other as her being 'the Star Trek girl' because she behaved like Star Trek's Kamala, 'the perfect mate'.[6] Kamala was an empathic metamorph who had the genetic aptitude to become whatever any man she is with most desires so that he will see her as his perfect mate. My client experienced several men apparently falling deeply in love with her, because with each one she metamorphosed into being what matched their fantasy of the ideal woman. But soon trouble would strike – she would become bored and seek someone new, or he would struggle when she tried to show parts of herself that were outside of the bubble he had her in.

The scariest part of becoming incorporated inside someone else's bubble is becoming annihilated – like with the Borg, your distinctiveness has been assimilated. But resistance may well not be futile.

If a person resists this, the incorporating person will be shocked, upset, offended, to realise that who they thought you were (i.e. a clone of themselves) is not true. If the relationship is of value to both of you, and there is enough basis there to be worth preserving, then you can fight for it. And fights there will be.

Successfully navigating this can lead to the optimal state for healthy and satisfying long-term relationships, which is shown in the third panel. In (c), each person has their own speech bubble intact, but there is an overlap between their respective bubbles. This means each has retained their own distinctiveness, each has their own personal views and interests, but each also shares an area with their partner in which they are in agreement or have stimulatingly compatible differences.

Another important aspect of panel (c) is that the lines of the speech bubbles are dotted. This means they are not solid, rigid, but are permeable. Each is open to being affected by the other, influenced by the other, flexible, an ongoing growing person in their own right and within their relationship to the other.

This overlapping area can also be called your comfort zone within that relationship. You don't have to have full overlaps in a relationship. As long as the overlapping area is satisfying enough to both of you, and you are mutually accepting and respectful of what is outside of the overlap, then you don't have to worry about what's outside of it. And you can potentially increase the size of that overlap over time. That overlap can also decrease over time, but maintaining a substantial enough area of overlap is what fuels the relationship.

Maintenance

The maintenance phase of a relationship is when flirtation has successfully led to consolidation, the various milestones of consolidation mentioned in the previous section have occurred, and a relationship has been established that both partners are fully committed to. The task then becomes maintaining this relationship.

Maintenance includes a continuing navigation of all the themes already mentioned, such as negotiating time spent together versus time spent apart, being a separate individual while also being part of a unit with your partner, and working to maintain 'detached engagement' and minimise projection. Negotiating sexual needs and interests is another area of importance. In all these areas, and throughout the life of a relationship, the three key aspects of relationship maintenance are:

1 Effective communication.
2 Effective conflict resolution.
3 Continuing mutual investment in the relationship to keep the overlapping area of shared engagement between you strong and active and mutually satisfying.

These maintenance tasks will be essential for managing the inevitable challenges, stresses, and changes that a long-term relationship will encounter, such as having children, managing work commitments, financial ups and downs, illness, parents' ageing, grown-up children leaving home, your own ageing. For your relationship to operate within the 'Thriving' quadrant, you want both partners to have a high percentage of freedom of self-expressiveness, together with acceptance from the other. Wherever possible, apply the principle of turning towards your partner instead of away from them. This means keeping them in mind, being inclusive of them, sharing yourself with them, and addressing rather than avoiding difficulties with them.

Effective communication includes continuing to use all the IT'S BETTER skills and also using the boxout guidelines from the previous chapters. This includes enjoying being playful with each other (Chapter 3), offering each other 'active listening' (Chapter 4), not being afraid of feelings (Chapter 5), appreciating the good interactions you have with each other and regularly letting each other know this (Chapter 6), and when there is a rupture between you, working actively to repair it (Chapter 7).

In any couple there will be times when conflict arises, whether this is ignored and suppressed (although it is never fully suppressed – if not explicitly expressed it usually just manifests in passive-aggressive behaviours), or at the other extreme, creates overt arguments that are destructive and at worst could even become violent. In couple arguments, a person with an avoidant style tends to withdraw, even walk away, whereas someone with an anxious style wants to get closer for reassurance and solve the argument there and then, feeling unable to bear the anxiety of not fixing it quickly.

A person with an anxious style might escalate the argument to try to get attention, to feel they matter to the other person, using protest behaviour like threats to leave in an attempt to make the other person beg them to stay, or attempts to make the other jealous. The avoidant style, on the other hand, might withdraw within a particular argument, or overall. Sometimes they can never fully invest in their current partner, occupying themselves instead with fantasies of finding the (more) perfect one, or by hankering after 'phantom X'[7] – becoming preoccupied with how great their ex-partner was and how much better a relationship they would have had with that person (who they didn't see as being so great at the time).

Instead of using such behaviours, more effective ways of dealing with conflict in a couple relationship involve using the same guidelines given in Chapter 7, 'Difficult conversations', particularly the section titled 'How to de-escalate and resolve conflict'. And when you experience there is a rupture, you can follow the guidelines in the Chapter 7 boxout on 'How to repair'.

Typical relationship issues for individuals with extreme intelligence

Domination and submission are not just S&M sexual practices but relate closely to the struggle that many very high-IQ individuals experience in trying to form romantic relationships. Given their typically strong-willed natures, they can run into problems with establishing a balanced way of relating that does not leave the other person feeling overridden. They can easily be at risk of becoming the person depicted on the left in panel (b) of Figure 8.1, subsuming the other person.

This can happen because a very high-IQ person often has a natural drive towards being in control. Also, they have a complex and racing brain which can take up a lot of their energy and attention, making it harder for them to make the genuine space that is needed for nurturing a partner's thoughts and feelings. Giving enough space to a partner might be something that does not come naturally but requires deliberate effort.

When this feels difficult, it's helpful to remind yourself why you want a relationship. Whatever is driving you to want a relationship can also be employed in motivating you to keep putting in the effort needed to make it work.

Issues with making space for someone in your life

Elon Musk told journalist Ashlee Vance, 'I would like to allocate more time to dating, though. I need to find a girlfriend. How much time does a woman want a week? Maybe ten hours?'[8]

Having a massively demanding work schedule is one way of finding it hard to make space for someone in your life, but another way is about giving them enough mental space, and yet another is about giving them a place in your life, in terms of a meaningful role.

If two partners live lives in which each is prioritising their own massively demanding work schedule, they will simply not have enough time to spend together to maintain a serious intimate relationship in which they stay involved with the details of each other's activities and thoughts and emotions and feel connected at a deep level. What seems to work – or even be necessary – is having a partner who is able to dedicate themselves to fitting around the very high-achieving person's demanding schedule. There are many high-profile examples of this. Quantam pioneer Paul Dirac, regarded as one of the most significant physicists of the 20th century, had a wife who supported him in this way.[9] Margaret Thatcher, the longest-serving British prime minister of the 20th century, had a husband who supported her in this way.[10] Corinna Schumacher went with her Formula 1 racing driver husband Michael Schumacher – one of only two drivers to win the world championship in that sport as many as seven times – everywhere he went, so that in whichever country he was competing she was there to spend with him whatever time he had off. She has spoken of what strength the comfort of that support gave him.[11]

Making mental space for a partner involves making space to keep them in mind, their interests and feelings and needs. This can be hard for an extremely intelligent person who is deeply absorbed in intellectually demanding work that preoccupies them around the clock – they might be 'there' with their loved ones but 'not really there' in terms of the attention they are able to give. In such a case the relationship will only work if their partner understands and accepts this.

Sometimes it is not preoccupying work that blocks out mental space for a partner, but a preoccupation with 'overthinking' things. An extremely intelligent person's highly active brain can rapidly create all sorts of possible reasons and meanings and speculations about what is going on with their partner, which can be imposed on the partner and overwhelm them, making the partner feel they are being told what they are thinking rather being given space to explain for themselves what they are thinking. When your brain races ahead, your partner can feel left behind. Deliberately practising the Titrate skill, and the Bridge skill, helps remedy this.

Giving a romantic partner a meaningful place in your life can also be a challenge. My client Karren[12] is superb at organisation and runs her home with well-planned precision. Her new partner had started spending a lot of time at her place and said that he had been wanting to make a contribution like buying things for her when they ran out, but nothing ever ran out. She told me, laughing, 'If he's waiting for that, it's never going to happen, because it's a system that's specially designed to work without relying on anyone else, and it's never going to fail!'

She is not the only very high-IQ client I have worked with who is so adeptly self-sufficient that a partner struggles to feel relevant because there is no gap they can fill, no room for something being needed that they are able to offer. It could be that running your life in such a self-reliant way is about wanting to ensure you are the one who stays in control.

Issues with control

Individuals with extreme intelligence can tend to take over because they're very capable. Also, they have often experienced they are right about things or are good at finding better ways of doing things. This can leave them with a strong belief that their way is best, which they can even extend to their domestic life with a partner.

An example is my client Hana,[13] whose husband would clean up after a meal by standing handwashing the dishes in the sink. She would criticise him and tell him to use the dishwasher instead. He would get upset and she found that incomprehensible – how could he be so inefficient when using the dishwasher would be faster! This is her being the bubble person, trying to subsume his way of doing things into her own.

Eventually he told her it had nothing to do with efficiency. He explained that he *liked* washing the dishes by hand. He liked the meditative slowness of it, of doing something relaxingly menial at the end of a long day's tough intellectual work. He liked the simplicity of the task and the satisfaction of being able to complete it there and then with his own hands and seeing immediate results, unlike his complex job in finance.

Hana had not been understanding what mattered to her husband, and her insistence that he should do things her way was damaging the relationship. Whether the way a partner is doing something is better, or worse, by whichever criteria you want to apply, or they're simply doing it that way because they like that, trying to control someone else to do it your way is like a minor act of violence and does not bode well for a relationship.

Sometimes a behaviour looks controlling but is more about taking over because of being too impatient to give the other person the time to do something that perhaps they will do more slowly than you are able to do it. I have a client whose partner was making a withdrawal from a cash machine, and she pushed in and took over because he was doing it too slowly. And yes, she could do it faster, but what does it do to the relationship that she has pushed in like that and made him feel inadequate? What are the gains in having acted that way? Has making that particular transaction faster been worth the longer-term damage it could have done to her partner's sense of self-efficacy in relation to her? In such situations, a partner is not being allowed to express their own potency to do things in their own way.

Issues with letting the other person have potency

By 'potency' I mean the capacity to be powerful. In an intimate relationship it can be hard to let your partner be exactly who they are, a whole other person who has power and freedom to think and say and do things which you cannot control but which will affect you because you are so closely involved with them. This can feel threatening. To feel safe one partner might subtly – or explicitly – begin to sabotage the other's potency, and not only sexually. Being disapproving of a partner, inhibiting them, trying to control them, neglecting them, or betraying them are all ways of sabotaging their potency.

If a relationship is pushed into a state where one of you is shut down, or both of you are no longer connecting deeply with each other (including sexually), or if you leave the relationship or drive your partner to leave, these are all ways of managing the fear of the other person's potency. 'Playing for safety' (see Chapter 3) by inhibiting a relationship or ending it prevents 'playing for enjoyment'. 'Playing for enjoyment' involves both of you being fully functional, potent individuals who choose to stay connected with each other on multiple levels because this enhances your lives.

A colleague and I had an interesting conversation, which we recorded, about a message she grew up with, communicated in often quite subtle ways, that 'smart women pay for their intelligence in their relationships'. She traced how this message was formed through three generations of her extended family's experiences, in which women who had become successful experienced their relationships suffering, often through their husbands' infidelity. They perceived that their male partners found their high ability threatening. In all cases the man cheated with a woman who was less educated and accomplished than his wife. From this my colleague deduced that for such a man to feel potent, he needed his partner to be 'less than' him, or show that she needs him, so he can be 'the hero'. My colleague grew up with her mother warning her about this.

> I always felt . . . this idea that I'm too much and I remember my mother telling me that a man wouldn't bear me, or what sort of man I should find who can bear me. . . . I do remember with this bloody PhD – it was . . . [laughs] . . . it was a burden in terms of relationships when I was dating. I had this weight of – if he's anything less than you then you'll have to pay for it at some point because he'll feel inferior and then he'll do something to put you down and it will be a power struggle, and it's never good for a marriage for the woman to be too smart because the man wants to feel in charge and it's emasculating or castrating if you are a successful woman.

We discussed whether intelligence and success were the main factors that caused these relationship problems and came upon the idea that a crucial factor is the way this is communicated. My colleague considered that when the successful woman did not show her partner that she cherishes him, he perhaps experienced being able to feel admired and cherished more easily with a partner who had less status and power than himself rather than more.

This makes me think of a high-achieving client of mine who was scathing about a new boyfriend having cancelled a date with her. She said, 'If he cancelled dates because he was at a sensitive point in his lab work that was finding a cure for cancer, fine, but – cancelling because he had to organise a drinks party for an exhibition?' She said this in a joking way with me, but this does communicate not respecting your partner's activities or concerns because you judge them as being of insufficient importance.

Communicating that you cherish someone includes letting them do things their way, giving them active listening, giving them a chance to articulate themselves, and if they do this at a pace slower than your own, not rushing forward with your high-speed brain to fill in all the gaps. Establishing roles for each other within your life together, where each person feels valued in their role, is important. As my colleague put it, 'Because if you want to be in charge in everything, then it's like you delete the other person'.

By truly allowing, rather than limiting, the other person's potency, you are not putting them in a cage. This means you get to feel the frisson of them choosing you when they come closer to you rather than expecting it as a certainty or a duty. In this way you sustain some of that sense of uncertainty and separateness and difference between you that exists during the flirtation phase of a relationship and which creates such exciting erotic tension.

Vulnerability

Not making space for a partner, wanting to stay in control, and sabotaging their potency can all be said to derive from one main underlying issue – the avoidance of vulnerability. All of these are ways of defending ourselves against our fear of how the other could hurt us.

If my client Karren lets her new partner take up a role in her life that she allows herself to rely on, and he lets her down or leaves, then she will have the discomfort of feeling lost, needy, and having to adjust to being without him. But she has already proven her capacity for self-reliance, so she can reassure herself that if this should happen, she will be able to adjust. It will feel difficult, unwelcome, uncomfortable, but these feelings are temporary and they are not feelings to be afraid of.

Embracing and communicating our vulnerability is a strength, not a weakness. This makes me think of a conversation with a client whose fiancé had behaved in a way that really upset her. She directed a lot of angry criticism towards him, spelling out to him what she felt he had done wrong. I invited her to tell me more about how she was feeling affected by how he had behaved. She became tearful, getting in touch with her feelings of vulnerability – her hurt at how he had behaved, her fear that he could hurt her again. I asked how she felt about the angry criticism she had directed at him. She said, 'I feel bad about that, I know that's not a good way to behave, but if I didn't show him my anger and tell him what he did wrong, how would he know that what he did was not okay?' I said, 'If you let him see that you are hurting, that is how he would know the impact of his behaviour. By showing him your vulnerability, that is how he would know.'

That was our last session before a summer break. In the next session, a month later, she told me that her experience in the previous session had been a breakthrough for her and had provided the turning point in how they were dealing with the rupture in their relationship: by expressing her vulnerability, her fiancé could connect with her rather than defending himself against her anger, and her example allowed him to express his own vulnerability also. She told me they were feeling closer than they ever had felt before.

Letting your partner learn to understand how you experience things involves using the Bridge skill to allow your partner to get closer to you. This involves showing them who you are, rather than telling them what to do. In this way you give your partner the compliment of building trust with them as the basis of feeling safe with them, rather than making an attempt to control them as the basis of feeling safe with them.

Each of us enters a relationship as Shakespeare's snail, afraid of a hit to our 'tender horns' that would cause us to 'shrink backward' into our 'shelly cave with pain', 'long after fearing to creep forth again'. But we are resilient, and we have our own potency. Maybe we don't have to be quite so afraid.

Do try this at home – Chapter 8 boxout

In a book about communication, I couldn't resist including a section that steps aside entirely from our typical reliance on using *words* for communication. And this chapter on intimate conversation – which is about relationships that include a physical dimension – is the perfect one in which to highlight the importance of communication that doesn't use words at all.

How to bond

When babies are born, the research-evidenced benefits of skin-to-skin contact between the infant and parent are emphasised for health and bonding (e.g. see Hubbard and Gattman, 2017). In adulthood, intimate relationship between couples is the context in which these same benefits can be experienced.

Loving physical touch stimulates pressure receptors under the skin. These reach the vagus nerve, which slows down the nervous system, putting you in a state of safety by reducing your stress levels and calming you. This kind of touching achieves co-regulation, releasing endorphins, which boost mood, and oxytocin, which promotes bonding (see Porges, 2017).

Skin-to-skin contact between adults is often associated with sex, but I'm recommending it in its own right, distinct from sex (whether or not it leads to, or follows, sex). It is something that is effective whenever comfort is needed. You can even try it during an argument: stop all the talking, and carry out the following instructions. These will help you reconnect with the deeper and more intimate feelings you share with your partner, which will put whatever the current argument is into a different perspective.

Instructions

1   Choose a place – perhaps your bed – where you feel comfortable, safe, private, and can fully relax.
2   You can do this at any time of the day or night. Decide with your partner how long you can both set aside for this exercise – to be effective, it should be at least 20 minutes, but it is great to do it for an hour. Set a timer, agreeing that you will be totally nonverbal with each other until the timer goes off.
3   Remove all your clothes.
4   Lie down together and hold each other, lying in a position that is comfortable and gives you as much full body contact with each other as possible (such as the spooning position).
5   Do not speak any words to each other at all, nor do anything at all. Simply lie still, holding each other close.
6   As you lie there, tune into what you are experiencing both physically and emotionally. Breathe. Feel the weight of your body relaxing into the bed. Notice what the contact of your partner's skin on yours feels like – the coolness of it, or the heat from it. Can you feel your partner's heartbeat or breath against you? How would you describe the scent or scents you are picking up? Notice the quietness between you. Then listen for what you can hear – background sounds, your own breathing, the sound of your partner breathing. See if you can bring your breathing in sync with your partner's. How does it feel being closely held like this? What emotions are stirring inside you? What thoughts are stirring inside you?
7   When the timer goes off, share with each other what that was like. Tell each other something you appreciate about each other that lying holding each other nonverbally like that put you in touch with. This might include gratitude for the trust between you that underpins your whole relationship and allows you to feel safe in each other's arms, naked.

If you enjoyed this exercise, you can even try a whole evening of being nonverbal with each other. This gives the bossy, rational prefrontal cortex a rest and encourages the intuitive, perceptive right hemisphere of the brain to come to the fore, which promotes bonding and 'gut feelings' about your partner that are more enduring than the regular rapid torrents of words that probably dominate your regular interactions.

Notes

1 Season 3, Episode 2.
2 Season 3, Episode 6.
3 Linehan (2015).
4 See, for example, Beattie (1992).
5 Falck and Shemmings (2014).
6 In Star Trek: The Next Generation, Season 5, Episode 21.
7 Levine and Heller (2011).
8 Vance (2012).
9 Farmelo (2009).
10 See the three-volume authorised biography on Margaret Thatcher, Moore (2013, 2016, 2020).
11 *Schumacher*, the Netflix documentary directed by Hanns-Bruno Kammertöns, Vanessa Nöcker, and Michael Wech.
12 For anonymity this is not her real name.
13 For anonymity this is not her real name.

References

Beattie, M. (1992). *Codependent No More* (2nd ed.). Minnesota: Hazelden Publishing.

Falck, S. and Shemmings, D. (2014). 'Fake It Till You Make It' – Can Deliberately Adopting Secure Attachment Behaviour Lead to Secure Attachment Organization? In D. Shemmings and Y. Shemmings (eds) *Assessing Disorganized Attachment Behaviour in Children – An Evidence-Based Model for Understanding and Supporting Families*. London: Jessica Kingsley Publishers, pp. 212–223.

Farmelo, G. (2009). *The Strangest Man*. London: Faber and Faber.

Hubbard, J.M. and Gattman, K.R. (2017). Parent-Infant Skin-to-Skin Contact Following Birth: History, Benefits, and Challenges. *Neonatal Network*, 36(2), pp. 89–97.

Levine, A. and Heller, R. (2011). *Attached*. London: Macmillan Publishers.

Linehan, M.M. (2015). *DBT Skills Training Manual* (2nd ed.). New York: The Guilford Press.

Moore, C. (2013). *Margaret Thatcher: The Authorized Biography* (Volume 1). Dublin: Allen Lane.

Moore, C. (2013). *Margaret Thatcher: The Authorized Biography* (Volume 2). Dublin: Allen Lane.

Moore, C. (2020). *Margaret Thatcher: The Authorized Biography* (Volumes 3). Dublin: Allen Lane.

Porges, S.W. (2017). *The Pocket Guide to the Polyvagal Theory: The Transformative Power of Feeling Safe*. New York: W.W. Norton & Company.

Vance, A. (2012). Elon Musk, the 21st Century Industrialist. [online] *Bloomberg UK Business*. Available at: www.bloomberg.com/news/articles/2012-09-13/elon-musk-the-21st-century-industrialist#xj4y7vzkg [Accessed 14 August 2022].

9 Occupational conversation (including office politics)

In my consulting work I repeatedly hear very high-IQ individuals express being baffled and bruised by workplace communication, saying that they do not understand what's going on around them or know how to manage it. Often they respond by avoiding contact with their colleagues and clients, becoming increasingly isolated and then despondent when it is someone else – with obviously lower ability – who gets promoted rather than themselves. These factors can combine to make them give up and leave jobs, causing ineffectual career trajectories that are disrupted and desultory.

Improving a person's communication skills can assist their high ability to be successfully channelled within an organisation for their mutual benefit. Better communication increases a person's effectiveness in any occupation, because every job has some element of having to deal with other people. In this chapter I will discuss this in the order of the typical sequence that engaging with an occupation involves, from the job-search stage onwards.

Throughout this chapter a very important difference applies in relation to everything I've said in preceding chapters about the Bridge skill. So far, I have talked repeatedly about 'giving away information for free' as part of how you build a bridge between yourself and others. But this chapter is about how you earn a living: in the occupational context, it's important to be very selective about what information you give away for free. Regardless of what your personal views are of your value, it is important to become savvy about what the market value is of what you are able to contribute. Respecting your own contribution, becoming wise about monetising it, and ensuring you retain ownership of it and get recognition for it are vital for earning a living.

Looking for a job: multipotentiality and locus of evaluation

Something that poses a challenge for people with extreme intelligence when considering the job market – which usually emerges long before specifically seeking a job – is multipotentiality. This means having the ability to do well in many different things. As a parent of a gifted child you go from one teacher to another on parents' evening and hear from each of them how excellent your

DOI:10.4324/9781003029106-13

child is in their subject and what extracurricular enrichment opportunities they can offer for further involvement and what a sparkling career could lie ahead for them in that subject. But there are only so many hours in a day: it is impossible for them to pursue everything they're good at. The problem is – how to choose?

This might seem a welcome problem to have, but it can be substantially debilitating. A person can become paralysed with options and not feel able to make a choice. They might be subjected to pressure from several directions to proceed with something someone else favours, making it hard to decide for themselves. They can find it hard to follow where their own interests lead them because of feeling so influenced by what others expect. For example, my client Ruby[1] described to me how she grew up with people being suspicious of her multipotentiality and the fact that she lost interest in things when she'd got what she wanted from them or they were no longer a challenge for her. That was seen as a lack of commitment, flighty, and also associated with risk – her parents scolded her that she wouldn't have a respectable life or income if she behaved like that.

Ruby introjected those views so strongly that by her forties she still found it impossible to feel positive about her multipotentiality. In social situations she avoided talking about herself, feeling there was something wrong and shameful about her various interests and that she really ought to be able to stick with just one thing. She also experienced that if she mentioned all her varied areas of strength she would be greeted with disbelief or treated as though she was boasting. It was a gradual process for her to begin accepting that she could design a life for herself which allowed several simultaneous involvements that represented her various interests and find ways of sharing this with others that would come across as factual and dignified rather than boastful or apologetic.

A key concept in helping such individuals to find their way with their multipotentiality is Carl Rogers's 'locus of evaluation'.[2] If you have an external locus of evaluation, you look to what others expect of you, being swayed by their views and desires, and acting in ways that are primarily driven by trying to win their approval or avoid their disapproval. Developing an internal locus of evaluation means shifting the emphasis from what others want of you to what you want of yourself, for your own reasons, whatever these are, and trusting those.

This doesn't mean ignoring others who are important to you. You're likely to always feel affected by how others view you and treat you, and you might live in a culture where the views of others like parents are especially powerfully imposed on you. But it does mean shifting the emphasis from trying to go along with their advice and wishes, to finding what your own purpose and meaning is in your life, and developing the courage to pursue that and communicate that to those around you. Using the IT'S BETTER communication skills can help with this, perhaps following the 'Difficult conversations' guidelines from Chapter 7. With the Bridge skill in particular you can try to understand where others are coming from and show respect for that but at the same time make it clearer to them who you are and what you feel and need and why.

One way of helping you find what you want to do is to undergo a CoreTalents Analysis.[3] This is an assessment tool specifically suitable for gifted adults because it recognises that you can have an unusually high number of strengths. Instead of simply identifying your strengths, as many assessments do, it analyses which activities generate joy and energy for you, compared with which ones deplete joy and energy from you. This helps you differentiate between things you are simply good at and those which positively add to your vitality. It starts by examining how you most loved playing as a child and works from there to provide a nuanced and complex report that identifies which activities are most beneficial for you as an adult.

If you really don't know what you want, I am a great believer in the usefulness of just doing something, starting somewhere, almost anywhere, and seeing that as a steppingstone. Doing any job at all, no matter what it is, rather than nothing, gives you experiences to process, lets you start getting to know about how something works, whatever it is, the tasks and routines and customs and interpersonal dynamics in that particular occupation. This gives you a position from which you can comment when assessing work practices and options, comparing the conditions you experience in one job with those in other occupations or fields, finding what is generalisable across jobs versus what is unique, and what stands out for you personally.

Also, everything you ever do can be made use of in some way. For example, as a young graduate J. K. Rowling worked for Amnesty International, where she had profoundly affecting experiences of human goodness and evil and the drive to power. Later she mined these experiences in her creation of the story of Harry Potter, which explored those themes in a way that has become a global phenomenon.[4] Steve Jobs talked about how looking back over his life he could join the dots of how even the most random-seeming experiences (like attending a calligraphy class after he dropped out of college) fed into what became his iconic contribution to the world (Apple devices with their beautiful typography).[5]

If you have a strong aptitude for something like maths, getting a degree in that gives you a foundation that can act as insurance against destitution, because it can later be adapted to a range of employment possibilities, whether a simple utilitarian income stream (like part-time tutoring or book-keeping) or a full-time accomplished career (such as becoming an actuary, economist, or a trader). In this way a foundational qualification in a core subject is a helpful start, because even if you don't use it later, doing it gives you the experience of applying yourself to something, persevering with something, and gives you a qualification that rubber stamps you as a suitable prospect for occupations that require some form of traditional educational foundation like having an undergraduate degree.

By recognising your high ability, you can use it to your advantage rather than expecting of yourself what is traditionally expected. For example, a client of mine has recently started searching for a post in her 'fall-back' area of expertise, which is corporate project management, to help finance her while she develops her preferred new occupation in the entertainment industry. She said, 'I'm applying for full-time positions but I know I will achieve everything they need of me in half that time, so I still have the time left over to pursue my real interests.'

You may have multipotentiality, but potential is not unlimited. At times you may have to mourn the loss of an opportunity or prior achievement. In her book *Gifted Lives*,[6] Joan Freeman gives an example of a gifted child who had exceptional talents in both science and piano playing. Should she pursue a career as an astronomer or a musician? On leaving school she went between the two without strong-enough application to succeed in either. Eventually she resigned herself to regular media attention as an example of a 'failed genius',[7] along the way becoming dependent on medication for depression.

Even if you have great success in an occupation, the world keeps changing – occupations that used to exist become obsolete. The human lifespan itself forces changes, and no-one is immune – you may excel to the level of winning Olympic gold, but then need to re-think your future when ageing ends your ability to perform.

This is where adaptability comes in – being able to recognise the change, mourn the loss, then activate yourself, with hope, to find something new. As Charles Darwin is credited with saying, it is not the most intelligent of the species nor the strongest that survives, but the one that is best able to adapt to change.[8]

Recruitment interviews

Once you have applied to almost any job, the possibility of gaining employment usually depends on first being interviewed. Job interviews are typically stressful conversations in which you are being evaluated for your suitability to be appointed to a position you might dearly want. How might you navigate this for the best chance of success?

I had a client – Alex[9] – who experienced huge disappointment when he learnt he had been unsuccessful at an interview for a sought-after post in a very high profile organisation that represented his dream job. I invited him to describe to me how the interview had gone. In his description, I picked up that in his attempt to convince the interview panel that he would be good at the job, he had taken up a stance of 'I'm better than you' (rather than 'I'm OK, you're OK'). He hadn't been aware of how his attempt to prove his prowess by being dominant might alienate the people he was trying to impress.

We talked about two different ways of approaching an interview. Method A involves trying to be an individual who will impress, trying to showcase what expertise you already have, and perhaps doing this in a way that tries to dominate and control the interview conversation, driven by a 'fixed mindset'[10] (this involves seeing yourself as having a limited quantity of value to offer, and expecting you will be judged on how good that fixed quantity of value already is). Method B involves demonstrating a capacity for moving from wherever you currently are towards something greater, wanting to be part of something bigger that you can make a contribution to, and participating in the interview conversation in a way that shows your ability to question, explore, and collaborate, driven by a 'growth mindset' (this involves seeing yourself as having an abundance of potential for learning and creating value, and expecting that you will be judged on how well you can demonstrate your capacity to keep applying yourself to tasks and problems and keep developing).

These insights proved transformative for Alex. About a year later he got another opportunity to apply for a job at the same organisation. This time, he very deliberately worked on approaching the interview with Method B, and he was successful. I loved seeing him getting to begin his dream job. (Dealing with the grudge he held against the first interviewers who had rejected him was a different aspect of our work.)

Using the Bridge skill helps with Method B. Instead of focusing hard on yourself as a separate commodity whom the interviewers are evaluating, show that you are also noticing who they are. You can do this by asking open questions about how they do things and making statements that demonstrate your wish to bring what you have to offer and adapt it in relation to who they are and what they need.

Individuals with very high IQ often tend towards using Method A, partly because they think their discrete individualism is their greatest value, and partly because they might have a dread around collaboration from previous difficult experiences of trying to work with others. Even if Method B attitudes are not (yet) strengths, if you can demonstrate them well enough to be given the job, then you can work on how to manage that further once you have started the job.

Starting a new job

The workplace environment – both physically, and culturally – has a huge impact on your effectiveness and well-being at work and beyond. A crucial aspect of this relates to Chapter 1's explanation of our physiology, and how at the unconscious level of neuroception we are always scanning for safety versus danger. Workplaces are often filled with low-frequency sounds (like air-conditioning systems, lifts) which our autonomic nervous systems pick up on as threatening, because this is the sound frequency related to the approach of potential predators rumbling in the undergrowth.[11]

Individuals with extreme intelligence are even more susceptible to finding noisy and harshly lit environments debilitating because they have heightened sensory sensitivity. One client told me how he absolutely couldn't bear the sound of his colleague chewing sandwiches in a shared office. Several others have expressed their genuine anguish to me when, for example, they've been seated in an open-plan office where the bustling conditions around them seriously disable their functioning. Taking your own needs seriously and communicating that you won't be able to your job in such conditions is much better than spending all your working hours in a physiological state of danger that gradually makes you ill.

The culture of a workplace has an equally big impact, and again safety versus danger is primary. Workplace cultures that try to set up fear of not performing well enough as a motivation to productivity can backfire when the kind of competitiveness engendered tips the balance from being inspiring into becoming threatening. Remember from Chapter 3 that 'playing for enjoyment' generates creativity and innovation, whereas having to 'play for safety' can paralyse. When people experience psychological safety, this induces feelings of vitality[12] and also makes them more ready to take interpersonal risks.[13] Research has demonstrated the power of healthy relationships at work[14] and proven that positive work cultures are more productive.[15] Harvard professor Amy Edmondson has become a vocal proponent for the benefits of 'building a psychologically safe workplace' (see her TED talk by that title). By practising the IT'S BETTER communication skills at work, you will be contributing towards these kinds of positive conditions.

Settling in at a job

Over and over again I hear from very high-IQ clients that soon after they settle into a new job they see how everything there could be done better, and say so. They find that people don't seem to be grateful to hear this, often ignoring what they've said. They cannot understand why – wouldn't people want to improve their work methods?

A client from Sao Paulo, Brazil, contacted me for coaching after he went through exactly this. He had become so baffled by why people around him were not seeing what he was seeing and why they were not understanding what he was trying to say or do that he went to a psychiatrist for help, fearing that maybe what he was experiencing as his good ideas at work were actually a form of delusional thinking he was suffering from. That consultation yielded an IQ test that showed his intelligence was in a very rare high bracket. This made him start thinking for the first time that maybe his insights and ideas were correct but others were just unable to follow his level of thinking. His work with me was to find how he could build a bridge between himself and these others.

Another client, Rob,[16] told his company how he could see where their industry was developing and how they could exploit this. He was ignored. Five years later, when he was utterly demoralised, bored, and disengaged and had started interviewing for new jobs, his company started talking about how to respond to what he had already told them five years previously. He soon got snatched up by one of the internationally biggest-name tech companies where the company culture has fully supported him to lead developments with his new ideas. But before that he went through years of distress from not being heard or understood and not being able to get traction with things he knew were important.

Sometimes the best solution is moving jobs, as Rob did, to a more conducive organisational culture. But sometimes shrewd communication can facilitate progress. I worked with a client on this for several months, focusing on how he could engage his company in a change he could foresee would be coming in his industry.

First, he began by finding out who the best person was to begin the conversation with. He showed them slides that I provided him with of the change process, to help address in advance fears that might come up for them (this represented the Soothe skill). He found out from key players what they would like to do about it next and discussed with them what procedure and pacing would suit them (this is the Bridge skill). He incrementally gave his message (the Titrate skill), leading to a snowballing of people becoming interested in what he was talking about. In this way, rather than becoming marginalised, he gained increasing recognition for what he was leading. Within a few months he sent me evidence of a triumph for him that this process had culminated in – a video of a presentation he made to the entire company. After months of active communication on his part, this represented being provided a platform of greatest visibility, because he had managed to successfully bring people along with him. Finding out who to deal with, when, and how is part of navigating office politics.

At the job: workplace dynamics or office politics

In this book so far I have encouraged the stance of believing the best of people. It's important to realise that sometimes this is naïve. I've emphasised taking the stance of 'I'm OK, You're OK'. In an episode of *The Simpsons*, the character Dr. Marvin Monroe refers to his self-help book *I'm OK, You're Sick and Twisted*. That joke is unfortunately sometimes the reality when it comes to people seeking profits and fighting for survival and dominance. 'Toxic workplaces'[17] can be populated with 'snakes in suits'[18] and the 'vicious combination' of 'psychopathy, machiavellianism, and narcissism'.[19]

Even without being subjected to sinister psychopathologies, very high-IQ individuals often find ordinary office politics daunting and stressful. A truth of many workplaces that such individuals tend to miss is that what goes on there is not all about – or sometimes, even mostly about – achieving the stated goals of the organisation. The reason this is missed is because many such individuals are highly task-focused and idealistic, with a natural leaning towards taking things at face value. As I have described,[20] they have

> a lack of artifice, [an] honesty, [a] strong moral integrity . . . [They are] unable to read the complexities, and [are] resistant to accepting the complexities, of the ordinary dissimulation of human social intercourse. This relates to [such individuals'] difficulty with conversation, in so far as conversation often involves avoiding or concealing, rather than engaging with, real issues.

Here are a few principles you can apply that will help with navigating office politics:

- *First and foremost, do not simply take things at face value.* Often what something looks like is not what's really going on (or not all that's going on). Expect hidden agendas, rather than being surprised when you come upon evidence of one. People do not always say/show what they feel and what they're really up to, and neither should you. For example, before disclosing something, consider what the worst is that could happen if you disclosed that and the situation was the opposite of what you'd imagined. Do you still want to disclose it?
- *Learn as much as you can about who has power, and what kind of power.* In Greek mythology Arachne boasts she can weave better than the goddess Athena. They compete and Arachne wins. Arachne can weave better, but Athena has more power. She transforms Arachne into a spider whose beautiful weaving will forever be simply dusted away. In your behaviour, be aware of what power lines are in place so you don't accidentally become electrocuted by them, and so that you go to the right place for energy.
- *Learn as much as you can about what motivates different individuals.* What is most important to someone might be different from what they publicly display as being important to them. Knowing what genuinely matters most to someone can make the crucial difference in whether a negotiation, for example, succeeds or fails.
- *Learn as much as you can about alliances between people.* With which person, group, or goal does a person's loyalties lie? For example, when someone seems to be illogically supporting a plan that goes against what you thought their values were, maybe something else is happening, like maybe they're secretly sleeping with the person who proposed the plan.
- *Build alliances.* Use the Bridge skill to learn who others are and show them you're noticing and thinking about how they might be experiencing something, from their perspective. Even sending a quick empathic text can have a strongly positive bonding impact. ('It looked like that was tough for you in that meeting trying to explain your request, it met with such resistance!')
- *Recognise the difference between public voice and personal voice.* People will say things 'off-record' that are different from what they will say 'on-record'. Open channels between yourself and others for 'off-record' conversations (this is part of the point of doing things which high-IQ individuals often dread and avoid like going out for drinks). You can also practice this by, for example, sending a formal email to someone which goes on-record, but separately talking to them, off-record, to let them know the email is coming (a Soothe skill), explaining to them where you're coming from and showing sensitivity to how they feel in the situation (a Bridge skill). Save the best of your humorous, critical, and controversial comments for off-record communications.

- *Sometimes it's better to prioritise the relationship or potential relationship over pure honesty.* During a conference, I (discreetly) walked out of a colleague's presentation when I realised it was the same one I'd heard them give before. The colleague completely changed towards me afterwards and I regretted it ever since. What were the relative merits of walking out to make better use of my time on that particular day, versus enduring something I'd heard before to make my colleague feel supported and protect a longer-term relationship with them?

- *Don't be Icarus.* Another good lesson from Greek mythology. Avoid flying too high when you're not robust enough (yet) to survive it (see the boxout at the end of the chapter about evaluating whether to take a risk).

- *Avoid splitting and projecting.* By this I mean avoid splitting yourself and others into good versus bad. A good antidote to criticising others is to remind yourself of times when you got things wrong or acted badly, and owning that, not projecting it onto the other as though they are the all-bad one and you are the all-good one.

- *Allow a margin for imperfection.* For yourself and others. Focus on strengthening things that work well, without expecting everything to work well. If you recognise you've made a mistake, admit it (follow 'Difficult conversations' guidelines, Chapter 7). If someone else has made a serious mistake that you need to address, follow the 'Feedback revisited' guidelines in Chapter 7. If something is very seriously wrong indeed, you might find yourself facing having to consider whistleblowing. But then that's usually the end of working at that job.

One of the ways of building alliances is to engage in networking.

Networking

What is networking? Until about ten years ago, I had no idea. When I did my executive coaching training, we had to get coaching clients to work with as training cases. I asked, 'How?' The reply was, 'Use your network'. As a psychotherapist I had never had to 'network' to get clients, so I didn't even know what that meant. But in a great many occupations, networking is central.

Essentially, networking is about sharing positive favours with others, and expanding the number of people with whom you can do this. The more people you meet and get to know something about, having a mutually positive exchange and sharing your contact details with each other, the more people you can draw on when a relevant situation arises.

So, how do you do it – how do you 'network'? When you meet someone, show goodwill towards them (the Soothe skill). Find overlaps of interest between you, which you can do by initiating giving away information about yourself for free and showing an interest in the other person, asking them open questions about themselves (the Bridge skill). Then be generous and give away favours that cost you nothing or not much. In a 'free association' kind of way (see Chapter 5), when they talk, think of who you know who has any kind of interest or involvement in something related to what they're talking about, and tell them about this, and offer to introduce them to each other. Other favours could be giving one hour of free professional advice for them or someone they know who needs it, or offering to sponsor their application to become a member of a club you belong to, etc. But keep it reciprocal between you (using the Titrate skill), both in content of conversation during your first meeting, and in actions over time if an acquaintance forms between you. In other words, don't keep giving if they are not also offering you generosity. When you get the hang of this, you can do it anywhere.

Small talk and improv (see Chapter 5) are also relevant to networking. The main difference with occupational networking is that you're thinking of how to create opportunities for the people you meet, or people they know, to buy your product or services (because this is not just about making friends but about having to earn a living). And whenever someone offers you something, thank them warmly and keep them in mind for how you can at some point reciprocate.

Disillusionment – locus of evaluation revisited

A client was telling me about a boss whom she really admired, and how this boss had told her some things that produced valuable learning for her and made a big difference in her career. She compared this with how many other people she's worked for 'are just idiots'. What made them idiots, she went on to say, was that they praised her for being excellent at things that in her view were completely trivial.

This made me think about how many people wish to find somebody they can trust and admire and learn from, and that for extremely intelligent people, finding this is rare. This is because having abilities in the top 2% of people gives them far fewer others who they feel truly challenged by. When they do, and that person appreciates them, it really means something. When what is easy for them is greeted by others as though it is an achievement, that is not satisfying for them.

This very understandable longing to find excellence that can guide you and challenge you is something you might also seek from a whole organisation. We want to believe in systems we can admire and trust and belong to, where everything works and is done well. It's a bit like being a child in a family, loving your family and wanting to believe they're the best, or at least that they're not getting it properly wrong and even harming you. How wonderful the bliss is of being in the state of accepting and feeling fully good about the system you're in – whether a family, or an organisation you work for, or a country you live in – and not needing to look outside of it for something better. How crashing the disappointment is when it lets you down.

I went to a climate change summit in which one of the panellists talked of her shock and disillusion at whole government systems globally when she learnt the facts on climate change. 'This couldn't happen, surely?' she described herself as having thought. 'There are grown-ups in charge somewhere who are making sure it will all be okay – they wouldn't let this happen, would they? We can trust the grown-ups?'

The search for a person, or an organisation, or a government, whom you will be able to fully admire and trust is ultimately another expression of an external locus of evaluation. Becoming disillusioned provides an impetus for making the shift to an internal locus of evaluation. This shift involves starting to set your own values and pursuing them by trusting in and investing in your own efforts and process of learning, regardless of what is happening around you. It involves moving from seeking 'A' grades in education to seeking the learning you personally want to gain from that education. It involves moving from looking to someone external who will make something of value happen, to looking how you yourself can work to make it happen. It is the shift from being an employee to becoming a leader. It is about making a place inside yourself where what you believe is good can dwell, all the values you hold true and wish to live by, and to make this the place you always return to for guidance.

The best articulation I've come across of how profound this principle is, is the words spoken by someone who had every reason to be in the throes of the most acute disillusionment possible. They are words spoken by Etty Hillesum, shortly before she was executed in a Nazi concentration camp[21]:

> You (God) cannot help us but we must help you and defend your dwelling place inside us to the last.

Do try this at home – Chapter 9 boxout

Different people will have very different perceptions of what constitutes a risk. And when you are faced with taking a possible risk, you might have months ahead to plan for it (like relocating to another country for a job), or it might be something you have to decide on in an instant (like making a trade on the stock market). The full sequence of steps in the following list is relevant when you have time to plan. If a fast decision is needed, you would go straight to step 5, and if an instant decision is needed, you would go straight to step 7, or even step 8, and you can later go back to any of the other steps that are still relevant.

How to take a risk

1 **List all the 'pros' and 'cons'.** Make a chart with two columns. In one column, write down everything in favour of the proposed action, and in the other, list all its possible drawbacks.

2   **Evaluate the extent of the risk.** What are the potential net gains? What is the worst that can happen if it goes wrong?

3   **Check whether it can be approached incrementally.** Is it an 'all' or 'nothing' option, or can you break it down into steps or stages? Can you buy yourself more time and the opportunity for trialling the course of action by agreeing on only the first stage, and after that negotiating about whether to commit to further stages?

4   **Plan contingencies for success and for failure.** What support might you need if it goes wrong? Is there insurance you can take out against failure? What support might you need if it succeeds?

5   **Prepare for action.** Discuss it with others if necessary or useful. Check you have researched the situation well enough. Where time allows, undertake any relevant training.

6   **Remind yourself of, and draw strength from, your 'stability zones'.** A stability zone (see Toffler, 1970) is an area in your life that will stay stable while other things around you are changing, and which supports and comforts you. Stability zones can be people or places or even pets that you love, groups you enjoy belonging to, meaningful possessions, values and beliefs that anchor and encourage you, and daily rituals (going to a favourite coffee shop, cooking, exercising, a good sleep routine) that give you familiarity and a sense of well-being.

7   **Take ownership.** When you are ready to make a choice of action, be clear that whatever anyone else has said or done or written, this is the moment at which you are yourself taking responsibility for your own choice.

8   **Breathe, be brave, and take the leap, trusting your choice and standing by it.** If it goes wrong, face it with dignity. Respect that you did your best in the circumstances you were in. Self-soothe, draw comfort from your stability zones, and begin learning from what happened. Make a plan, or follow the plan you already made, for failure. If the choice you made goes well, enjoy that and celebrate. Acknowledge and show your gratitude to others who helped make it possible. Make a plan, or follow the plan you already made, for success.

Notes

1   For anonymity this is not her real name.
2   Rogers (1959, 1961).
3   See van de Ven (2022).
4   Rowling (2008).
5   See Isaacson (2011).

6 Freeman (2010).
7 Freeman (2010, p. 184).
8 Darwin Correspondence Project (n.d.).
9 For anonymity this is not his real name.
10 Dweck (2006).
11 See Porges (2017).
12 Kark and Carmeli (2009).
13 Edmondson and Lei (2014).
14 Seppälä and McNichols (2022).
15 Seppälä and Cameron (2015).
16 For anonymity this is not his real name.
17 Kusy and Holloway (2009).
18 Babiak and Hare (2019).
19 James (2013).
20 Falck (2020, p. 203).
21 In Gans (2003, p. 4).

References

Babiak, P. and Hare, R.D. (2019). *Snakes in Suits*. New York: HarperBusiness.
Darwin Correspondence Project. (n.d.). *The Evolution of a Misquotation*. University of Cambridge [online]. Available at: www.darwinproject.ac.uk/people/about-darwin/sixthings-darwin-never-said/evolution-misquotation [Accessed 15 May 2019].
Dweck, C.S. (2006). *Mindset: How You Can Fulfil Your Potential*. London: Constable & Robinson Ltd.
Edmondson, A.C. and Lei, Z. (2014). Psychological Safety: The History, Renaissance, and Future of an Interpersonal Construct. *Annual Review of Organizational Psychology and Organizational Behaviour*, 1, pp. 23–43.
Freeman, J. (2010). *Gifted Lives: What Happens When Gifted Children Grow Up*. London: Routledge.
Gans, S. (2003). *The Little Book of Goodness*. UK: Lightning Source UK Ltd.
Isaacson, W. (2011). *Steve Jobs*. London: Little, Brown.
James, O. (2013). *Office Politics*. London: Vermilion.
Kark, R. and Carmeli, A. (2009). Alive and Creating: The Mediating Role of Vitality and Aliveness in the Relationship between Psychological Safety and Creative Work Involvement. *Journal of Organizational Behavior*, [online] 30(6), pp. 785–804. doi:10.1002/job.571.
Kusy, M. and Holloway, E. (2009). *Toxic Workplace: Managing Toxic Personalities and Their Systems of Power*. San Francisco, CA: Jossey-Bass.
Porges, S.W. (2017). *The Pocket Guide to the Polyvagal Theory: The Transformative Power of Feeling Safe*. New York: W.W. Norton & Company.
Rogers, C. (1959). A Theory of Therapy, Personality and Interpersonal Relationships as Developed in the Client-Centered Framework. In S. Koch (ed.) *Psychology: A Study of a Science. Vol. 3: Formulations of the Person and the Social Context*. New York: McGraw Hill.
Rogers, C. (1961). *On Becoming a Person: A Therapist's View of Psychotherapy*. London: Constable.
Rowling, J.K. (2008). *Very Good Lives*. New York: Little, Brown and Company.
Seppälä, E. and Cameron, K. (2015). Proof That Positive Work Cultures Are More Productive. [online] *Harvard Business Review*. Available at: https://hbr.org/2015/12/proof-that-positive-work-cultures-are-more-productive.

Seppälä, E. and McNichols, N.K. (2022). The Power of Healthy Relationships at Work. [online] *Harvard Business Review*. Available at: https://hbr.org/2022/06/the-power-of-healthy-relationships-at-work [Accessed 16 July 2022].

Toffler, A. (1970). *Future Shock*. London: Pan.

Van de Ven, R. (2022). *Giftedness in Practice*. Holland: Big Business Publishers.

10 Dealing with change (including gaining success)

When clients with extreme intelligence book sessions with me, it appears they are doing this because they want something in their life to be different from how it is. In the first session they tell me of x or y or z that's bothering them and causing difficulty or substantial suffering. But soon – sometimes even in that first session – they say they are worried that if that thing gets solved and a change is made, they will lose some important essence of themselves that would destroy their capacity to work in the way they do.

I worked with an internationally successful and award-winning theatre director who was afraid if he lost his misery, then, along with it, he might lose his creativity. I worked with an award-winning television producer who recognised that the strategies he had developed for coping with his personal fears and limitations had worked well for him professionally; he had really profited from them. One client told me that when he was at his most cynical and disappointed and disgusted by what he saw in the world around him, that was also when he was most able to eloquently comment on that and satirise it, or provide a critique that was poetic and inspired. He feared if he didn't have the depths of despair, then he would no longer have the provocation and impetus which gave him his best work. Another client talked about how when he was most angry he would become hyper-articulate, with a strong intensity of energy that came out in a verbalisation of his views that was uniquely expressive.

I say to these clients, you don't have to worry about this. The world will always continue to find ways of disgusting you. There will always be another opportunity for becoming incandescent with rage. Just by remaining alive you will again be faced with new sources of challenge and suffering. You are who you are, your essence will persist, and your talent will take whatever you experience and create work out of it. But if you're overall happier and enjoying yourself more and you're better able to collaborate successfully with others, then that can be expected to increase rather than harm your productivity. There is not a single case I've worked with for whom improving their self-awareness and knowledge and finesse in interpersonal communication did not produce significant benefits for them.

These reservations they initially express – the paradox of booking a session to pursue change but then being afraid of what it might entail – are part of

DOI:10.4324/9781003029106-14

the natural human wariness of change. Underlying this is the same principle of seeking safety and avoiding danger: the familiar situation, however much suffering it involves, feels safer than the unknown of what you'd be dealing with if it changed. This chapter focuses on dealing with change, especially with regard to gaining success.

Change causes dysregulation

A person might seek therapy because there's something they think they want to change, but the process of therapy itself often represents an unsettling change for clients with extreme intelligence who have become strongly self-reliant. They tend to have experienced themselves as highly effective in many areas of their lives, often singled out for how their abilities and achievements surpass those of others, and they are strong-willed, wanting to do things their way and having a strong conviction that their way is best.

Mathematician Sergei[1] consulted me for help with forming a long-term romantic partnership. He had never been able to make an attempted relationship last beyond a few months and was longing to share his life with someone and develop a stable sexual relationship. He told me how he was going about meeting someone and would describe dates to me. When I commented on any aspect of his approach, he would give me a lot of well-reasoned arguments for why he had done something that way and how that detail fitted with his overall strategy for securing a partner. Eventually I said, 'Okay – but it's not working! What's the point of paying me to keep justifying to me why you're doing everything the way you are when it's not working? Don't you want me to help you come up with something different you can try that could work?'

Relinquishing being fully self-reliant in his therapeutic relationship with me began Sergei's evolution towards becoming able to relinquish full self-reliance with someone else, which was central in enabling deeper involvement for him with a romantic partner. It was a challenging but rewarding process: by the end of our work together he had moved in with a partner, having moved far beyond the ways in which he had previously been stuck.

Allowing yourself to get emotionally close to someone, or be helped by someone, can feel threatening to your autonomy. You might feel afraid that this means you are less competent or effective than you thought you were, because someone else has come up with something you hadn't already thought of yourself. If being self-sufficient has been a cornerstone of your self-worth, along with a fear of needing anyone else, then the possibility of changing this can trigger dysregulation. To regulate yourself and try to restore a feeling of safety, you might try to defend yourself against change (as Sergei did, arguing and justifying as a way of resisting how uncomfortable it felt to change the things he was familiar with).

The larger a change is, the more dysregulating it will be. Whether it is a change that is awful or beyond-your-wildest-dreams wonderful, you can expect to need time to take it in and become regulated before you will feel grounded again. Some tips on 'How to ground yourself' appear in the boxout at the end of this chapter.

Holding back from success

When a person has extreme intelligence, there is often the expectation that their high ability will ensure they succeed in whatever they might set their mind on. This expectation in itself affects how a person lives with their extreme intelligence. For example, the expectation of success might motivate their efforts and drive their confidence, which can make them more likely to succeed, but this can also mean that any experience of setback or failure is so unanticipated that it is disproportionately debilitating, making it harder to bounce back. Or, others' expectations that they will succeed could be experienced as such a burden that the person disengages from setting any goals for themselves and making any effort at all.

Becoming successful in many contexts often involves – or even requires – becoming a leader. Even when a person wants to take up a leadership role, sometimes they also dread it. And in this case, they can be in conflict with themselves, saying they want a leadership role but sabotaging their chances of attaining it. They can do this by signalling to others, in ways they may not even be conscious of, that they are not ready to become a leader. Such signals can include the following:

- Regularly deferring to others.
- Frequently seeking permission/protection/validation from others.
- Being overly cautious and tentative in contributions you make.
- Lacking decisiveness.
- Spreading yourself thin across many areas without developing authority in any one area.
- Keeping your work 'behind the scenes' and not letting others know how you have made a contribution.
- On occasions when you do discuss your work, minimising your effectiveness/capability/influence.
- Being passive rather than proactive – waiting to be noticed/promoted/told what to do rather than initiating progress and directing it.
- Not knowing, or not communicating clearly, what you are able to do and would like to do and how it can benefit others.
- Not working to build relationships with others that would make them trust you and want to support you.

There are many reasons why people with very high IQ might be susceptible to these behaviours. These include the following:

- Perfectionism – not being willing to start something or complete it unless you can perfect it to your high standards.

- Imposter syndrome – not believing you are entitled or adequate to take on a position and fear of being found lacking.
- Fear of failure – not wanting to try in case you don't succeed.
- Fear of disappointing others' expectations. Fearing you will not be able to sustain the standards they expect of you or the performance they have previously praised you for.
- Fear of success and the pressure and responsibilities that come with it.
- Lack of effective communication skills for initiating things, reaching out to people, self-advocacy.

Recognising these ways in which you might be holding yourself back from success might in itself be enough to help embolden you to make a change. If a person with extreme intelligence stops holding themselves back, and if they combine their high ability with good communication skills together with solid preparation in terms of knowledge and skill, and if they demonstrate confident direction and motivation, you would expect such a person to succeed. Such an outcome might be expected to be desirable and lead to happiness. But success is a change that can be difficult.

Success: change in status

Why did musician Amy Winehouse repeatedly say she didn't want to be successful? 'Success' is often something people fantasise about and strive for. Winehouse said that if she became a success she would 'go crazy, insane, top myself or something'.[2] I wonder what she meant by that, how she perceived success, what she feared.

What happened to her is that she did achieve extraordinary success, with fame, money, and awards, together with the most nightmarish of problems with alcohol, drugs, eating, love, and eventually her ability to perform. All of this unfolded before the strobe-light flashes of the paparazzi who ceaselessly pursued her, and ended in her death by alcohol poisoning at the age of 27. At the end of the documentary on her life by director Asif Kapadia, her bodyguard poignantly reports that she had acknowledged to him her incredible musical talent and said that if she could 'give it back' in exchange for being able to just walk down the street without being harassed, she would.

Being harassed was a change in how Winehouse was treated by others, and it was an unwanted change resulting from her success. What any success, or failure, has in common is change. Fantasised positive change is what makes success something desired and sought after. And negative change – whether brought on by success, or failure – is what is feared, struggled with, or avoided.

Change brought on by success and failure often involves gains or losses in status, meaning changes in how we are perceived, and treated, by others. You might gain higher status through accomplishing a milestone achievement or gaining promotion or winning awards, and you might experience diminished status through failure, loss of position, ageing. Either way, a change in status can lead to changes in responsibility, income, lifestyle, the people one associates with, and a changed sense of self. But how is this related to extreme intelligence?

Success, intelligence, and tragedy

The doctor who spoke to Winehouse the day before she died called her 'one of the most intelligent young women I've ever met'.[3] Higher intelligence is strongly correlated with achievement in all fields, as established by large bodies of research.[4] But it is also well-evidenced that when intelligence enters the highest bands of extreme intelligence, its relationship to successful achievement can become inverse.[5]

There are many reasons for this, some of which are easy to find representation of even in general journalism. For example, Lindsay Miller, who interviewed Kapadia, described Winehouse as 'scary smart'.[6] She wrote that Kapadia told her, 'I think there was a word [Winehouse] used a lot: bored. She was just so clever'. He described that her friends would be playing some children's game like hide-and-seek and would find her in a corner not joining in, reading things like *Schindler's List* at the age of eight. Kapadia said, 'I think that was part of her problem, the intelligence.'[7] So here the fact that she had high intelligence was quickly portrayed as a difficulty: 'scary' (threatening to others), alienating (she'd be set apart, on her own, not joining in with others), and causing dysregulation (feeling bored is an uncomfortable state to be in that a person will search for ways to get out of).

Success leading to tragedy is not uncommon. In addition to Kapadia's documentary on Winehouse and her stardom as a musician, he made documentaries on Formula 1 racing driver star Ayrton Senna and footballer star Diego Maradona, who both also met tragic ends. Kapadia used a powerful fly-on-the-wall methodology to show how success affected these individuals.

But this is not the story of every success. For each successful person in these fields who met a tragic end, counterparts can be found in the same field who have also been successful but who have lived or are living longer lives, and lives which remain within the bounds of greater safety. Such a counterpart for Amy Winehouse is another supremely successful musician, born three years after Winehouse's birth, who also has extreme intelligence but who has not 'crashed and burnt' and is still going strong. Her name is Stefani Germanotta, professionally known as Lady Gaga.

As an adolescent Lady Gaga was selected to attend an enrichment programme at the Johns Hopkins University's Centre for Talented Youth.[8] The entrance criteria for that programme were not only having to score in the top 1% at university entrance exams but also taking those exams at an age five years younger than average. Looking at the contrast between tragedy and ongoing success in these two highly intelligent young women who gained fame within the same field begs the question of what makes the difference.

The answer will be that a great many factors are involved, and the question is one that can be delved into with extensive research. I will consider it here by exploring a few key differences I have observed between Amy Winehouse and Lady Gaga, based on watching documentaries on each of these two musicians. Kapadia's documentary on Winehouse[9] came out four years after her death, in 2015, and two years later, in 2017, a documentary came out on Lady Gaga, using the same fly-on-the-wall methodology, directed by Chris Moukarbel.[10] Such documentaries obviously do not provide a comprehensive study of their subject, and they remain frozen in the moment in time at which they were made, so my intention with the observations I make here is that they be treated not as conclusive statements about the lives and works of Winehouse or Gaga but as a starting point for further exploration and discussion of the associated themes.

Looking after your own health

One of the first scenes in the documentary on Lady Gaga shows her in her kitchen, appreciatively tasting a healthy-looking salad being prepared for her and then cooking for herself. She is paying attention to her own health – taking care of her basic needs for nutrition. She glows with being in peak physical condition, her body fit and strong.

Throughout, she pays attention to the physiological demands on her of her career. She has several practitioners who hover around her, ready to give a massage when needed, a facial, a cold press. However talented she is, she still has to do her vocalisation exercises, think about what she eats, and remain hydrated – all the little physical details that support her performance.

During a medical consultation, her doctor says that in order for Gaga to do her job, she has been willing her body to perform, shutting down her emotions and physical pain. Gaga talks about how she hadn't realised she'd been doing this. She demonstrates the process of learning she is involved in about how her body and mind work, how an injury has affected her, how her motivation to gratify her fans affects her, producing adrenalin that drives her and gives her strength to perform in spite of pain. She continually seeks advice, voluntarily, on the most suitable treatments that will support her well-being and accepts the assistance others offer her with this.

By contrast, the documentary on Amy Winehouse charts her progression from a fresh-faced, robust, and healthy-looking teenager to a weak and emaciated figure less than a decade later whose physical health and vitality has been destroyed. The focus of what she consumes is not on nutrition but on alcohol and various drugs. Rather than seeking learning about and assistance with her well-being, she created one of her most famous songs as an expression of her disdain for the advice she was given to go into rehab ('No, no, no'[11]). Eventually she accumulates so much toxicity in her body that it kills her.

The crowning public appearance of the Gaga documentary is her triumphant halftime performance at the Super Bowl LI to rapturous applause and critical acclaim. The crowning public appearance of the Winehouse documentary is the concert in Belgrade, Serbia, where, waif-thin, she wanders around on the stage, looking disoriented, and doesn't even begin the performance she was contracted to give. The confused audience start shouting angry insults and booing her, and the concert – and rest of the European tour it was meant to kick off – is terminated.

The entertainment performance industry is brutally demanding, competitive, and exploitative, with a 'systemic culture of injury and pain tolerance'.[12] Many injuries are from 'overuse' rather than accidents. But that is not the only industry that will use workers as an expendable commodity and disregard their well-being. It is up to the individual to look after themselves. Without concerted *self-care* there can be no ongoing success for any individual, no matter how talented.

Your attitude to success and fame

Whatever Amy Winehouse meant when she said she didn't want success, once she became successful, her attitude appeared to remain consistent and she made several displays of her hatred of it. She looked terrified of her fans, like she was prey being hunted down, and regularly would become angry and physically lash out in attacks against the paparazzi who surrounded her. That Serbian concert – it could be her psychological and physical collapse that stopped her from performing, but it could also have been her antipathy towards her admiring audience, her contempt for being expected to sing the same songs over and over again, which made her rebel and refuse to do it. She commented on how boring concerts were for her if she wasn't high.

By contrast, Lady Gaga seems to embrace her success with interest, creativity, and gratitude, taking it in her stride. She is clearly directing the laser of her extreme intelligence at the phenomenon of fame, observing it, questioning how it works, learning about it, playing with it. Instead of behaving as though it is something unwelcome being imposed on her, she uses her own agency to engage with it. She talks of how she can see what people want of her, such as to be sexy or a receptacle for their pain, and describes how she will interact with that by putting an absurd spin on it, so that she stays in control. She calls that a 'methodology'.

Gaga, like Winehouse, is also subjected to her audience's strong demand that she keep performing in the same way she always has done. But rather than becoming oppressed by this and simply going along with it or rebelling by refusing to perform at all, she experiments with it. In Moukarbel's documentary, we watch Gaga navigate an image change, and she discusses her awareness of the risk she's taking in imposing change on her fans. Taking such risks, though, is what keeps her art fresh for herself. Again this demonstrates how she stays in control, remaining centred in her own agency. She has become known for regularly reinventing herself and her musical (and then acting) repertoire.

The way Gaga relates to her fans is also very different compared with Winehouse. She regularly expresses gratitude for them, interest in them, and an attitude of caring for them. She talks about them being her 'heart and soul'. The documentary shows her meeting with a fan and learning up close what her music means for that individual. She lets the conversation touch her, becoming tearful. The conversation brings mutual connection and reward. In this way Gaga converts her view of her fans from an anonymous mass audience tormenting her to individual persons who are having a personally significant experience of her.

Overall, Winehouse appeared to experience her success as though she was an exploited victim, whereas Gaga takes control of her success and *she* becomes the one who exploits *it*, 'playing for enjoyment'. Maintaining ongoing success seems to rely on the individual adopting an attitude in which they are not passive victims of circumstances but act from a clear sense of their own *agency*. But what makes one person able to embrace this attitude, and another not?

Relationships

How we function is powerfully impacted by how the relationships in our lives sustain us or deplete us. The first subject Lady Gaga mentions in the opening scene of the documentary is relationships. She talks of being lonely. Echoing the theme from Chapter 8 of managing 'potency' within an intimate relationship, Gaga raises the issue of how women becoming powerful affects a relationship with a man and asks how he can be comfortable and secure enough to find his own way with that. She ascribes her previous relationship failures to this issue, noting that every breakup coincided with a career milestone – her accomplishment of something pivotal that marked her entry into a higher bracket of success.

Although Gaga was single at the time of the documentary and lonely for a lover, she was clearly deriving a lot of valuable support from family, friends, and the people she worked with. She names her family as the most important thing in her life. There are scenes of her attending family events, spending time with her parents and grandparents, sharing laughs and hugs. She is seen giving regular pep talks to her entourage. She thanks them and validates them with comments of how important they are to her and how much she appreciates them. And she even turns her fans into a support network, notably with a song (*Hey Girl*) whose lyrics urge women to make life easier by 'lifting each other up' rather than competing against each other.

By contrast, the Winehouse documentary shows relationships in her life that deplete her and bring suffering rather than support. Friends speak of how they became alienated by her self-destructive behaviour. Her turbulent six-year relationship with Blake Fielder-Civil, to whom she was married for two years, is widely blamed for her irrevocable path to deterioration and ultimate catastrophe. By all accounts he was responsible for introducing her to drugs, and in the documentary, he is described as being 'on the gravy train' with her, using her wealth to enable his drug habit.

Winehouse also had disappointing experiences with her closest family members. There is a poignant scene with her father, whom she apparently adored and whom she invited to visit her in St Lucia, where she'd gone for a restorative break. When he arrives, he has a camera crew with him. Ostensibly they are filming him on his trip to the island, but as Winehouse remarks to him, it is not him who is newsworthy, it is her who they want to gain access to via him, and he has gone along with it. There is such a sense of the lost little girl about her, and a sense of how her heart sinks when she realises that her father's supposed investment in spending time with her is ultimately a betrayal of her.

Without close others who have your well-being at heart, who remain loyal to you and provide protection, empathy, encouragement, and companionship, it is hard to remain strong. Being able to embrace success might not be possible without having an effective *support network*.

The focus of your work

Another difference apparent between Winehouse and Gaga in the two documentaries is the focus of their work. Musically, both are exceptional talents. But the subjects of Winehouse's songs focus on narrowly personal experience (often despair-driven) like drug addiction and sexual betrayal, whereas Gaga's are not only personal but also extend beyond herself to connect with wider themes like fashion, fame, feminism. She also connects her work with her family history.

In the Gaga documentary she is preparing her new album *Joanne*, named after a deceased aunt. She pores over memorabilia with her family, being interested in and moved by Joanne's history. In this way she makes evident her capacity to think about and care about someone else's experience, making that the focus of her work.

Beyond her own family history, she also connects with historical figures like women accused of being witches and burnt at the stake. In this manner she moves away from only focusing narrowly on herself to exploring her personal experiences within wider contexts. She describes how she employed her 'methodology' in her performance of her song *Paparazzi* at the 2009 VMAs (MTV Video Music Awards). She was happy to be the sexy performer others wanted of her, but in addition she ensured that she also reminded her audience of what fame did to stars like Marilyn Monroe. She did this by ending her performance hanging from a noose covered in fake blood.

In these various elements of the Gaga documentary there is a theme of what things mean to her. She shows what her family means to her when she shares old family stories with them as though they matter and preserves family relics. She finds meaning in her fans' connections with her. She makes meaning in her songs and performances, linking these with the plights of historical figures and wider contemporary themes. She is constantly in the process of thinking about meaning, connecting with meaning, making meaning.

Noticing this made me think of the work of psychiatrist and philosopher Viktor Frankl. During the Second World War he spent three years imprisoned in four different Nazi concentration camps. He became fascinated by what the difference was between prisoners who fell into despair and gave up, resigning themselves to death, and those who kept fighting hard to survive. He found that those who were able to endure the terrible conditions they were in always had a purpose beyond themselves – a child or spouse they longed to see again, believing a day of liberation would come that would reunite them, or an unfinished task or creative work that they felt driven to return to. He concluded that having a meaning to live for is what saved them.[13]

When looking at Amy Winehouse and Lady Gaga, who both had great success, but one catapulted herself to a premature death whereas the other is still surviving and thriving, I wondered whether it is this same insight of Frankl's that makes the most profound of the differences between them. If meaning is what saves those who are in concentration camps and have nothing, perhaps it is also *meaning* that saves those who are famous and have everything.

How to cope with the dysregulation of change

The discussion so far in this chapter has yielded four main principles for helping with regulating yourself and staying well through the changes that success can bring: self-care, agency, support network, and meaning. *Self-care* emphasises that all of us, even superstars, are made of muscle and bone and organs. No matter what is happening in our lives, we need to take care of our own biological necessities to stay well.

Agency highlights the importance of becoming the author of your own actions. You do this by centring yourself on goals you have chosen, then from that core, actively engaging with opportunities. It also means exerting influence and retaining control of how you participate in what's going on around you.

Support network means recognising the importance of the people around you. Make careful choices to surround yourself with people who will sustain rather than deplete you. Then make regular efforts to nurture those positive relationships, staying in touch with what's happening in their lives, spending time together, sharing your life with them.

Meaning is about why you do something or what or who you do it for. Immensely successful and prolific novelist Stephen King describes how he writes his books for his wife, Tabby.[14] She is the first reader of every book he writes, and when she has started reading a new manuscript, he watches her and waits for the moment when she will hopefully laugh at something he's written.

> I love it when Tabby laughs out of control – she puts her hands up as if to say I surrender and these big tears go rolling down her cheeks. I love it, that's all.[15]

And that's what he does it for.

It's not the abstract concepts of success of failure in themselves that hold power, it is the associated changes. If you can manage change, you don't have to worry so much about either success or failure. You would then, as Rudyard Kipling wrote, be able to 'treat those two impostors just the same'.[16]

Do try this at home – Chapter 10 boxout

In the context of living with extreme intelligence, grounding yourself doesn't mean being prevented from flying. It means that even when you have taken off and are flying, it is necessary to schedule in intervals where you will come back down to the ground again. This is because you need to land to refuel, do a maintenance check, rest, and stock up to be ready for the next flight. Without doing these things, if you try to just keep continuously flying, you will crash.

How to ground yourself

- **Place both of your feet fully on the ground.** Then breathe. Follow the instructions on 'How to breathe' in the Chapter 1 boxout.
- **Think of how every single thing is broken up into steps.** You knit a whole jumper one stitch at a time. You write a whole book one word at a time. You climb a whole mountain one step at a time. When you're at the bottom of the mountain, you know you have a goal of reaching the summit, but you don't have to worry now about how you will take that last step up to the top. For now, what you must focus on is the next step, the one that gets you started up the slope. If you keep focusing on and taking each next step, while keeping the end goal in mind, you will automatically get to the goal.
- **If you feel demoralised that where you are right now is not nearly far enough, look at where you have come from.** Congratulate yourself on the distance you have already covered, and value and be grateful for what you have managed to achieve so far.
- **If you don't feel entitled to be in the position you've achieved, remind yourself that you got it because you were ready for it.** Remember the steps you took to get there. Appreciate that these prepared you for where you are now. Believe that your journey so far has qualified you to be exactly suited for where you are now.
- **If you find yourself feeling arrogant about where you've got to, look ahead to where you need to go next.** See your current achievement as a normal step along your journey, acknowledging

that it is great to have got to this step, but think about the goals that lie ahead and what the step is that you'll be taking next.

- **Remind yourself that however successful you are, there is someone who is more successful than you.** Think of someone whose achievements have surpassed your own, to put your individual situation into perspective. What inspiration can you take from them?
- **Remind yourself that however bad things are for you, there is someone who has it worse.** Think of what you can still be grateful for. Even if you have failed at something, still you are not a malnourished orphan who is alone and terrified in the wake of a tornado that destroyed your entire home and family. Is there someone in need who you can help?
- **Remind yourself that however good or bad things are, every day you need to take care of your own biological existence.** You will still get thirsty and have to drink, get hungry and have to eat, get tired and have to sleep. You need to exercise to keep your body healthy and fully functioning – strong, supple, agile. You need to keep clean: every day bodily odours will build, and bacteria will accumulate in your teeth, and these will become a problem if you don't attend to them.
- **Remind yourself that up until the day that you die, tomorrow is another day.** Tomorrow you can try again – you can do more of the tasks on your list, work to repair something that went wrong, and work to build something good. And however much you have achieved today, tomorrow you will have to do a lot of it again – you will have to Soothe again, Bridge again, Titrate again, and every day you will have to feed yourself again, sweep the floor again, brush your teeth again, sleep again, every single day. And that's okay.

Notes

1 For confidentiality that's not his real name.
2 Quote by Amy Winehouse in 2015 documentary *Amy*, directed by Asif Kapadia.
3 Sky News (2012), quote by Dr Christina Romete.
4 See Falck (2020), e.g. p. 116.
5 See Falck (2020), e.g. p. 116.
6 Miller (2015).
7 Miller (2015).
8 Clynes (2016).
9 *Amy*, documentary by Asif Kapadia.
10 *Lady Gaga Five Foot Two*, documentary by Chris Moukarbel.
11 *Rehab* by Amy Winehouse.
12 Mainwaring et al. (2001).
13 See Frankl (1959).

14 King (2000).
15 King (2000, p. 218).
16 Poem *If* by Rudyard Kipling.

References

Clynes, T. (2016). How to Raise a Genius. *Nature*, 537, pp. 152–155.

Falck, S. (2020). *Extreme Intelligence*. London: Routledge.

Frankl, V.E. (1959). *Man's Search for Meaning*. London: Rider.

King, S. (2000). *On Writing*. London: Hodder & Stoughton.

Mainwaring, L., Krasnow, D. and Kerr, G. (2001). And the Dance Goes On: Psychological Impact of Injury. *Journal of Dance Medicine and Science*, 5(4), pp. 105–115.

Miller, L. (2015). *5 of the Most Fascinating Details About the Amy Winehouse Documentary* [online]. Available at: www.popsugar.co.uk/celebrity/5-Most-Fascinating-Details-About-Amy-Winehouse-Documentary-37841426 [Accessed 30 July 2022].

Sky News. (2012). *Amy Winehouse Inquest to be Reheard*. 17 December [online]. Available at: https://news.sky.com/story/amy-winehouse-inquest-to-be-reheard-10460513 [Accessed 30 July 2022].

Concluding comments

In the introduction, I talked about how effective communication can break barriers: the barrier of not making a relationship you want, the barrier of not being able to say what you need to, the barrier of not knowing how to manage conflict. This book acts as a primer to help you break those barriers.

I am aware that what I have presented here is a lot to take in, and yet I have so much more material which there isn't space to include, and so much more to say on all the content that I have included. I'm also aware that what I've written is to some extent by definition superficial or simplistic, because writing can only ever be an approximation of the reality involved. Dealing with the lived experiences of splitting, of projection, of the visceral fear or anger you feel when your autonomic nervous system goes into a state of defence, all of this is exponentially harder than the way I've written about it can convey. It is so hard that psychotherapists take years to learn how to deal with it in their clients, and more years to fully understand it themselves, and a lifetime to keep grappling with how to manage it within their own relationships.

All people with extreme intelligence face a learning curve to get to understand the nature of themselves and how that relates to others. They are in a minority so it's harder to find people similar to themselves. But they are still the same as all others in that they do seek relationship, they are significantly benefited by finding connection with others that is full of acceptance and safety and which creates joy and well-being – others with whom they can love playing – and they are seriously affected, like anyone, very negatively by rejection and isolation.

Because very high-IQ people are used to the power their minds have, they can be susceptible to thinking they can get whatever they want, fix whatever they want, make whatever needs to happen, happen. The dominance of rational thinking in the Western world reinforces this attitude by making us think everything is controllable, but it's not. There are a great many things, and arguably the best things in life, that cannot be willed. You cannot with the power of your will force someone to be happy, to play, to sleep, or to fall in love, or have an orgasm, or conceive a child.[1]

A supervisee talks with me about a profound journey she has been going on with a client of hers who has advanced cancer and has been having gruelling

DOI: 10.4324/9781003029106-15

treatment. My supervisee is accompanying her client as she faces fear, pain, arrangements with her family for when she's not there anymore, finances, death. My supervisee describes how moving she has been finding this experience, and asks for my help with what she can say or should not say in conversations as difficult as these. The answer? Tune. Soothe. Bridge. Titrate.

She asks me what my views are on death. We talk about the mystery of life and death, quantum mechanics, Buddhist meditations on decaying and ceasing to exist in your currently known form, Edna St. Vincent Millay's poem *Renascence*. Living with uncertainty.

At the end of the session I say to her, 'What was it like for you asking me that, and how did you feel about my response?' (That's me asking for feedback, facilitating reflection on not just the content we shared but also the process of what having the conversation had been like.)

She says, 'Amazing. It was amazing just being able to ask you that straight up.'

Being able to say anything to someone else, ask anything, express anything, and experience interest from them, attention, and acceptance is very freeing. The more freely you can express yourself, and experience others' acceptance, the more you thrive. Conversation is brain-changing, and even one conversation on its own can be life-changing.

I wonder whether you've had a conversation that changed your life? If you'd like to let me know, feel free to write to me.

Ah but there goes the doorbell now – it's my next client, and I look forward to the next conversation.

Note

1 See Farber (2000).

Reference

Farber, L.H. (2000). *The Ways of the Will*. New York: Basic Books.

Index

Note: Page references to Figures will be in **bold**. Footnotes will be denoted by the letter 'n' and Note number following the page number.